AN EVENT-BASED SCIEN

FIRST FLIGHT!

STUDENT EDITION

Russell G. Wright

DALE SEYMOUR PUBLICATIONS®
Parsippany, New Jersey

The developers of Event-Based Science have been encouraged and supported at every step in the creative process by the superintendent and board of education of Montgomery County Public Schools, Rockville, Maryland (MCPS). The superintendent and board are committed to the systemic improvement of science instruction, grades preK–12. EBS is one of many projects undertaken to ensure the scientific literacy of all students.

Montgomery County Public Schools

The developers of *First Flight!* pay special tribute to the editors, publisher, and reporters of *USA TODAY* and *NBC News*. Without their cooperation and support, the creation of this module would not have been possible.

Managing Editor: Catherine Anderson
Senior Editor: Jeri Hayes
Production/Manufacturing Director: Janet Yearian
Production/Manufacturing Manager: Karen Edmonds
Senior Production/Manufacturing Coordinator: Roxanne Knoll
Design Manager: Jeff Kelly
Text and Cover Design: Frank Loose
Cover Photograph: Smithsonian, Museum of Americn History.
Catalog number 86-14937
Student Photographs: EllaJay Parfitt

This book is published by Dale Seymour Publications®, an imprint of Pearson Learning.

Dale Seymour Publications
299 Jefferson Road
Parsippany, NJ 07054
Customer service: 800-872-1100

This material is based on work supported by the National Science Foundation under grant number ESI-9550498. Any opinions, findings, conclusions, or recommendations expressed in this publication are those of the Event-Based Science Project and do not necessarily reflect the views of the National Science Foundation.

Printed in the United States of America.

Order Number 29816
ISBN 0-7690-0025-8

DALE SEYMOUR PUBLICATIONS®

This product is printed on recycled paper

2 3 4 5 6 7 8 9 10-ML-03 02 01 00

Contents

Preface

The Event-Based Science Model

First Flight! is a unit on the physics of flight that follows the Event-Based Science (EBS) Instructional Model. You will watch videotaped news coverage of the historic flight of the *Voyager*. It made the first round-the-world trip by an airplane using only one tank of gas. You will also read authentic newspaper accounts about aviation and the aviation industry. Your discussions about the video and articles will show you and your teacher that you already know a lot about the physical-science concepts involved in flight. Next, a real-world task puts you and your classmates in the roles of people who must use scientific knowledge and processes to design an airplane. You will probably need more information before you start the task. If you do, *First Flight!* provides hands-on activities and a variety of readings to give you some of the background you need. About halfway through the unit, you will be ready to begin the task. Your teacher will assign you a role to play and turn you and your team loose to complete the task. You will spend the rest of the time in this unit working on that task.

Scientific Literacy

Today, a literate citizen is expected to know more than how to read, write, and do simple arithmetic. Today, literacy includes knowing how to analyze problems, ask critical questions, and explain events. A literate citizen must also be able to apply scientific knowledge and processes to new situations. Event-Based Science allows you to practice these skills by placing the study of science in a meaningful context.

Knowledge cannot be transferred to your mind from the mind of your teacher, or from the pages of a textbook. Nor can knowledge occur in isolation from the other things you know about and have experienced in the real world. The Event-Based Science model is based on the idea that the best way to know something is to be actively engaged in it.

Therefore, the Event-Based Science model simulates real-life events and experiences to make your learning more authentic and memorable. First, the event is brought to life through television news coverage. Viewing the news allows you to be there "as it happened," and that is as close as you can get to actually experiencing the event. Second, by simulating the kinds of teamwork and problem solving that occur every day in our work places and communities, you will experience the roles that scientific knowledge and teamwork play in the lives of ordinary people. Thus *First Flight!* is built around simulations of real-life events and experiences that affect people's lives and environments dramatically.

In an Event-Based Science classroom, you become the workers, your product is a solution to a real problem, and your teacher is your coach, guide, and advisor. You will be assessed on how you use scientific processes and concepts to solve problems and on the quality of your work.

One of the primary goals of the EBS Project is to place the learning of science in a real-world context and to make scientific learning fun. You should not allow yourself to become frustrated.

Student Resources

First Flight! is unlike a regular textbook. An Event-Based Science module tells a story about a real event; it has real newspaper articles about the event, and inserts that explain the scientific concepts involved in the event. It also contains science activities for you to conduct in your science class and interdisciplinary activities that you may do in English, math, or social studies classes. In addition, an Event-Based Science module gives you and your classmates a real-world task to do. The task is always done by teams of students, with each team member performing a real-life role while completing an important part of the task. The task cannot be completed unless you do your part. The team approach allows you to share your knowledge and strengths. It also helps you learn to work with a team in a real-world situation. Today, most professionals work in teams.

Interviews with people who actually serve in the roles you are playing are scattered throughout the Event-Based Science module. Middle school students who actually experienced the event tell their stories throughout the module too.

Since this module is unlike a regular textbook, you have much more flexibility in using it.

- You may read **The Story** of the event for enjoyment or to find clues that will help you tackle your part of the task.
- You may read the **Discovery File** when you need help understanding something in the story or when you need help with the task.
- You may read all the **On the Job** features because you are curious about what professionals do, or you may read only the interview with the professional who works in the role you've chosen because it may give you ideas that will help you complete the task.
- You may read the **In the News** features because they catch your eye, or as part of your search for information.
- You will probably read all the **Student Voices** features because they are interesting stories told by middle school students like yourself.

First Flight! is also unlike regular textbooks in that the collection of resources found in it is not meant to be complete. You must find additional information from other sources too. Textbooks, encyclopedias, pamphlets, magazine and newspaper articles, videos, films, filmstrips, computer databases, and people in your community are all potential sources of useful information. It is vital to your preparation as a scientifically-literate citizen of the twenty-first century that you get used to finding information on your own.

The shape of a new form of science education is beginning to emerge, and the Event-Based Science Project is leading the way. We hope you enjoy your experience with this module as much as we enjoyed developing it.

—Russell G. Wright, Ed.D.
Project Director and Principal Author

THE STORY—PART 1

Dreams of Flight

For eons, when they looked up at the sky and watched birds soaring above their heads, people have dreamed of flying. Legends and myths about flying machines and superhumans have always made imaginative stories.

With flapping wings on their arms or with their bodies dangling beneath crude gliders, people tried to fly. Throughout the centuries—including the 19th—their attempts failed. Not until the 20th century did humans finally conquer the air, as they had the land and water.

It was exciting to be alive at the end of the 19th century. In the 1890s, bicycles were becoming popular. Electricity was beginning to light up America's homes and streets. People talked to each other on the recently invented telephone, and a few people drove the new gasoline-powered wagons called automobiles. But human flight was still a dream.

Inventors in Europe were working on aviation experiments during this time. But it would be two American brothers from Dayton, Ohio, who would invent a machine that could really fly. It was the Wright brothers who launched the Age of Aviation.

PHOTO COURTESY OF HENRY FORD MUSEUM & GREENFIELD VILLAGE, THE EDISON INSTITUTE

The Wright Cycle Company

PHOTO COURTESY OF THE SMITHSONIAN INSTITUTE

Wilbur and Orville Wright

With a mother who enjoyed tinkering and fixing things, and a father who encouraged them to explore and experiment, one might say that the Wright brothers had designer genes; and the idea of flying had long fascinated Wilbur and Orville. When their father, a bishop in the church, brought them a flying toy, they tried to copy it and make it bigger.

But in 1889, the brothers put aside their dreams of flight to try the printing business. Orville dropped out of high school to join his brother Wilbur who was already out. They played around with old printing presses and built their own out of used parts. Orville and Wilbur began printing a weekly newspaper. After about a year, with their paper failing to thrive, the Wright brothers changed the focus of their business. They called their new company Wright and Wright, Job Printers. They took in all kinds of general printing jobs.

Then the bicycle craze hit. Since their neighbors knew the Wright brothers were good mechanics, they started bringing their bikes to the print shop for repair. In 1892, Orville and Wilbur hired someone to run their printing business and they opened the Wright Cycle Company. At first they sold, rented, and repaired bicycles. Later they built them.

At this time, the brothers became interested in photography, especially the work of German-born Otto Lilienthal. Lilienthal built and flew gliders, until 1896 when a gliding accident killed him. News of Lilienthal's glider experiments reawakened the brothers' dreams of flight.

PHOTO COURTESY OF THE SMITHSONIAN INSTITUTE

The Wright Flyer

Using their knowledge and skills as bicycle mechanics, Orville and Wilbur Wright started tinkering with kites and gliders. They built them in the back of their shop. But to test their ideas, they needed a place with predictable winds, and soft ground for landing. In 1899, they found the perfect site—a remote beach on the North Carolina coast near the town of Kitty Hawk.

Orville and Wilbur assembled their glider at the Kitty Hawk beach in 1900. It would be a few more years and several crashes before they would build a successful flying machine and really take to the air.

At around the same time, another inventor, Samuel Langley, was also working on gliders. The Army awarded Langley a huge sum of money—$50,000—to develop a steam-powered version of his aircraft. Most people assumed that if anyone would win the race to be the first to fly, it would be Langley.

In December of 1903, at the highly publicized demonstration of his steam-powered "aerodrome," Langley and his aircraft catapulted off the roof of a houseboat. Instead of soaring into the sky, Langley and his invention dove into the icy waters of the Potomac River. Langley survived the crash, but he and his ideas were now out of the running. He resigned from the Smithsonian in disgrace, taking his dreams with him. Those who had believed and invested in Langley's ideas looked like fools.

The day following Langley's dunking, the *New York Times* stated that a "man-carrying airplane would eventually be built—but only if mathematicians and engineers worked steadily for the next one million to ten million years." Nine days later, Orville Wright took off!

PHOTO COURTESY OF THE WRIGHT STATE UNIVERSITY

Wilbur in the bicycle shop, 1897

Discussion Questions

1. **Have you ever flown in an airplane? Describe the experience. Can you remember the sounds, smells, and feelings on your first flight?**
2. **Explain how an airplane can stay up in the air.**
3. **If you needed to travel to a city about 1,000 miles away from your home, would it be safer to fly or drive?**
4. **If you were going to build an airplane, what features would you want it to have?**

Taking to the Air!

Congratulations! You're a new aeronautical engineer, and you just *landed* a job with a company that designs and builds airplanes. Today, when you walked in the door, you saw this message posted on the bulletin board:

> **ENTER THE AIR SHOW**
>
> **The Air Show is looking for new airplanes to exhibit.**
>
> **Fly your airplane in front of thousands of spectators!**
>
> **Talk to potential buyers!**
>
> Meet buyers from commercial airlines, air freight carriers, private pilot organizations, the federal government, and more!
> Become the fastest growing aeronautical company with the most advanced planes!
>
> ENTER NOW!

What an exciting idea! This sounds like an event you can't pass up.

But, wait! You're not the only one who's new here. The company is new. You and your colleagues have never worked together! How could you possibly be ready in time? After a long talk, you and your colleagues decide that being new shouldn't hold you back. All it will take to win is an airplane that works well, carries its crew and passengers safely, and reaches out to a part of the market that no one else has tried to reach.

Important people will attend the Air Show. They are people interested in buying the best designs. Imagine someone coming up to you and saying, "I'd like to buy 100 of your airplanes." You and your partners would become rich overnight!

But there's more to entering the Air Show than just building the airplane. Visitors need to see what your creation looks like on the inside. A poster showing the aircraft and its interior may do the trick. When people come along and show interest in your poster, you can point to it and say, "Isn't that a beauty? Imagine yourself in the cockpit of this baby!" Who knows, one of the people who sees the poster may be ready to offer you a big contract!

Someone from the Federal Aviation Administration (FAA) may show up and ask hard questions. She will probably want to know if your plane is safe. No one will want to buy a design that hasn't been proven to be safe for crew and passengers. Make sure you have diagrams that show the planes safety features. It also takes data and graphs to convince people that the safety features actually work. A safety engineer will make sure your plane is safe.

Remember the last time you went to a new car dealership. You picked up that little booklet that told about the your favorite car. It was so convincing! It made you want to buy that car! Wouldn't it be great to be able to hand out a flashy brochure to anyone who shows an interest in your plane? Maybe your brochure will impress a rich entrepreneur who will come back after reading it and say, "I'll take fifty." A marketing engineer is just the right person to prepare that brochure.

In this task you will work with your team to design and build a model of a future airplane. You must be ready to display your plane at the Air Show in five weeks! There you will be asked to fly your plane, make it do a number of maneuvers, and show that it's safe.

The Roles

You and your team members will each submit a prioritized list to your teacher. Indicate your preferences (first choice and so on) for your roles. First choices will be assigned if possible. Read over the Job Descriptions before deciding on your preferred role. Make sure you are willing and able to meet the responsibilities of the role. If there are things about the task that your group does not know or is not yet ready to do, please let your teacher know.

Job Descriptions

During the design and construction of the airplane, each engineer will keep a detailed log of the work.

All the experts are expected to know the parts of an airplane and have a thorough understanding of airplane design and the four forces that work together to keep an airplane in the air; but for this task other knowledge and skills are also needed. Of particular importance are *wing shape* and *angle of attack.*

Chief Aeronautical Engineer will:

1. lead the work of the team, using the Preliminary Design Review and Critical Design Review worksheets (from the teacher) as guides.
2. supervise the design process, constantly checking wing shape and attack angle.
3. decorate the plane for display at the show.

Design Engineer will:

1. work with the chief aeronautical engineer on design, flight testing, and evaluation. (Pay special attention to control surfaces.)
2. keep careful records in the Testing Log. (Provided by the teacher. The Testing Log should contain diagrams and comments on how the airplane is put together and results of all experiments and flight tests.)
3. make a poster showing the interior and exterior of the finished aircraft.

Safety Engineer will:

1. work with the aeronautical and design engineers to make sure the aircraft is safe for humans.
2. prepare a display showing safety features of the aircraft.
3. make sure that all safety features are working at the Air Show.

Marketing Engineer will:

1. lead the team in the selection of the type of plane you are designing and the audience of potential buyers.
2. use tradebooks, encyclopedias, the World Wide Web, and other resources to research your competition for the market you have selected.
3. design a flashy brochure about your airplane and its features. Be sure to highlight the ways it's better than the competition.

Building Your Model

When you and your teammates have all the knowledge and skills needed to complete the task, you are ready to start. You can begin to plan and build a model of the plane you will enter in the Air Show.

First, agree on a type of airplane you will build. What will be its purpose? Who will buy your plane? Make a sketch of your final idea. Taking careful notes of all discussions and record them in your log.

Before starting to build the plane, your team must complete a PDR (Preliminary Design Review form) and submit it for approval. The PDR will ask you about: the materials you plan to use for a model of your plane, the jobs your plane is designed to do, and the number of people it will carry.

After your PDR has been approved, carefully build a model of your aircraft. Test it as soon as you can. You may find that your plane doesn't fly very well. If that happens, review the lessons you learned in each of the science activities. Are you applying the principles to your model? If you decide to scrap your old design and start with a new one, complete a new PDR and have it approved.

When your creation is almost ready, it must pass the dreaded Critical Design Review (CDR). Can your *bird* really do what you think it can do? Can it make a left turn? Can it make a right turn? What about landing safely? No one likes a crash landing at an air show. How far can it go? A long flight will really impress everyone looking on. If your team fails the CDR, you will have to revise the design and try again. But there isn't much time.

The Big Event

Finally, the time comes. The Air Show is here! Time to get your airplane ready to exhibit, to set up your poster, to show all the safety features, and to have that attractive brochure ready. Let the show begin!

Good Luck!

ON THE JOB

Air Safety Investigator

MARGARET NAPOLITAN
MANAGER OF AIR SAFETY INVESTIGATION AND RECORDS ADMINISTRATION
THE NEW PIPER AIRCRAFT, INC.

When I was a little girl, my father rented a helicopter and had the pilot take us for a ride. I thought it was so much fun looking down on the beautiful scenery and flying through the air, I fell in love with flight at that moment. I became intrigued with why airplanes fly. In high school I studied math and physics and started flying as soon as the law permitted—at the age of 16.

The math and physics I studied in grade and high school allowed me to understand the concepts of flight and gave me the knowledge I needed to study Aeronautical Engineering in college.

After college, I went to work as a flight test engineer testing airplanes for Douglas Aircraft Company, Long Beach, California. My work as a flight test engineer forced me to think about the safety of flight. In the field, while testing an airplane design, we identified problems and had the authority to change its design. As a Safety Analyst, you are expected to have knowledge about the product to have

the foresight to change the product so it will not hurt anyone.

To become a Safety Analyst, studying your subjects thoroughly is important. You must be able to think analytically. This is not easy. Studying math and physics will give you the tools to be able to identify and analyze a problem and come up with solutions to solve that problem.

When you are working with your team to design your airplane for the Air Show, others on your team might resist the changes you want to make for safety purposes. Be persistent and have data to back up your changes.

When designing an airplane, the team must ask, "How safe is safe enough?" Airplane manufacturers have the challenge of designing a product that the public perceives is safe.

One safety technique we use when designing our airplanes is to put redundant systems into the aircraft. For example, we put two of the same flight instruments in the cockpit. If one instrument fails, the pilot can use the other one.

Also, in the aviation arena, we examine all airplane crashes and try to find out what caused the crash. During the accident investigation, we reconstruct the airplane wreckage and the events around the accident, such as weather at the time and location of the accident. Analyzing these facts may indicate the cause of the crash. We do this to learn more about why airplanes crash so we can prevent other crashes and hopefully save lives.

When you're doing the science activity, *Out to Launch*, and first throw your paper airplane, it may fall to the ground without going anywhere. By trial and error (considered flight testing in the manufacturing world), you will bend certain surfaces on your airplane to see if that particular change makes your airplane fly farther and longer. You will observe and document the results of each trial flight. Through this analytical process, you will design a safe and better paper airplane. You have just become a Safety Analyst.

IN THE NEWS

Anxiety-grounding programs take fear out of flying

After high-profile crashes, seminar enrollment soars

By Laura Bly
USA TODAY

Less than a week before Mae Westbrook arrived at the Minneapolis-St. Paul airport to take her first airplane trip in 25 years, TWA Flight 800 plummeted in flames into the Atlantic Ocean.

The morning of her flight, a local newspaper announced its reporters had breached Northwest Airlines' security to roam freely through the carrier's maintenance hangars and cargo areas.

Such unfortunate timing might have prompted another white-knuckle flier to tear up her boarding pass — or spend the flight downing a couple of Bloody Marys.

But Westbrook, whose hour-long jaunt to Chicago represented the culmination of a Northwest-sponsored weekend program for fearful fliers, was unfazed.

Until she took the course, "my legs would buckle if I even thought about getting on an airplane," says Westbrook, a 69-year-old grandmother who signed up after her children moved to Florida.

By the end of her two-day stint, "I realized that fear of flying isn't a fear of dying . . . it's a fear of losing control."

That fear, which affects an estimated 1 in 6 Americans, seems more palpable this summer as airlines ratchet up security efforts in the wake of the TWA crash. And while many jittery fliers continue to mask their anxiety with booze or tranquilizers, a growing number are turning to programs like Northwest's for help.

Though budget cuts prompted American and USAir to discontinue their fearful flier seminars, calls to Northwest's Wings Freedom to Fly program have doubled since the ValuJet crash in May. At Denver-based Flight Without Fear, meanwhile, inquiries have jumped from two or three a month to three or four per day.

"It works both ways," says Lisa Hauptner of Westport, Conn.-based Seminars on Aeroanxiety Relief, also known as SOAR. One of about 35 programs nationwide run by therapists, pilots and airlines, SOAR has seen inquiries double since the ValuJet and TWA crashes heightened the concerns of white-knuckle fliers.

But, Hauptner adds, some would-be participants use headlines about watery graves and maintenance lapses to buttress and justify their reasons for staying home: "It's the 'I told you so' factor."

Hauptner and other experts say most anxious fliers ask for help because they're reluctant to give up control to an unseen pilot and crew.

"If I don't like the way someone's driving, I don't have the option of getting out at 30,000 feet," says Wendy Gasinski, 28, a staff assistant from suburban Chicago. She signed up for a fearful flier program this summer after her new employer told her to get over her apprehensions or find a job that didn't require travel.

Many other white-knuckle fliers suffer from claustrophobia or a fear of heights, or develop their phobia after a major event such as a parent's death, job loss or birth of a child. And some are grounded by a negative flight-related experience such as a missed approach or bout of turbulence.

No matter what the cause, fearful flier seminars take a similar approach to a cure: stress management, deep breathing exercises and other relaxation techniques, coupled with a nuts-and-bolts emphasis on the mechanics of flight. Most programs include a short "graduation flight" and claim a success rate of 90%-95%.

Along with detailed discussions on hydraulics and landing gear, instructors cite the industry's safety record. One favorite statistic, from the Massachusetts Institute of Technology's Sloan School of Management: If you took a commercial flight every day for the next 29,000 years, odds are that you'd be involved in one commercial airline crash.

"People are always asking me about my most terrifying moment, and I tell them I haven't had one," says Tom Bunn, a 30-year United Airlines captain who directs the SOAR program. "Of the hundreds of pilots and flight attendants I know, no one has been injured in an accident."

Statistics aren't much comfort when it comes to terrorism, admits Glen Arnold, a licensed pilot and aviation psychologist based in Newport Beach, Calif.

"Safety concerns crop up on a regular basis, going back to the Chicago DC-10 crash (in 1979)," Arnold says. "Terrorism has a much broader impact. It's like the bogyman in the closet. . . . You can't corner it or get a handle on it, and it's a painful reminder of our own vulnerability."

But, he adds, "We try to get across that to be alive is to be vulnerable. . . . There's no way to guarantee safety, even if you're holed up in your house."

USA TODAY, 14 AUGUST, 1996

STUDENT VOICES

I was excited, nervous, and scared about flying. At first, my stomach felt nasty. But I got used to it and loosened up. If I designed an airplane, I'd leave off the cargo area. You don't really need it.

JENNIFER EDWARDS
BALTIMORE, MD

IN THE NEWS

Where to find help to conquer air-travel phobia

A sampling of resources designed to help turn chickens into eagles:

▶ **Northwest Airlines' Wings Freedom to Fly.** Weekend seminars are held monthly in Minneapolis and other cities served by Northwest; $450 includes graduation flight. Information, 612-726-7733.

▶ **The Institute for Psychology of Air Travel.** A Boston-based, 11-week group counseling program, including graduation flight, costs $300. The institute's Web site (http://www.ads-online.com/InsPsyAir/) includes tips and lists of other fearful flier resources. Information, 617-437-1811.

▶ **Seminars on Aeroanxiety Relief.** Course includes audiotapes, booklets and two-hour counseling session by phone for $390. Information, 800-332-7359.

▶ **THAIRAPY.** Aviation psychologist Glen Arnold offers periodic seminars in Southern California; a self-help book and relaxation tape costs $30. Information, 714-756-1133.

▶ **Flight Without Fear.** An eight-week, Denver-based program, including graduation flight and session in a United Airlines flight simulator, costs $375; next session starts Sept. 24. To register: 303-278-4435.

▶ ***The Fearful Flyers Resource Guide*** (Argonaut Entertainment, $19.95). Barry Elkus and Murray E. Tieger, a pyschotherapist, describe more than 35 seminars, self-help tapes and books aimed at fearful fliers. To order, send $11.95 to Argonaut Entertainment, 455 Delta Ave., Cincinnati, Ohio, 45226.

Some tricks to keep flight fright at bay

Tips for fearful fliers from the Institute for Psychology of Air Travel:

▶ **Plan.** Choose a forward aisle seat on a wide-body plane to minimize noise and allow freedom of movement.

▶ **Watch what you eat.** Cut back on caffeine and sugar the day before your flight, and never take off on an empty stomach.

▶ **Get to the airport early.** Since rushing to make a flight can produce its own anxiety, plan to arrive at least 1½ hours beforehand for domestic flights and 2½ hours for international flights, giving you enough time to go through security.

▶ **Don't be shy.** Let the flight attendants know you're a fearful flier, and ask the crew for a pre-flight peek into the cockpit.

▶ **Try to relax.** Deep-breathing exercises and relaxation tapes (available on several airlines' audio channels) can help.

▶ **Remember the odds.** Your chances of dying in an airplane accident are 1 in 4.6 million vs. 1 in 125 that you'll die in a car crash.

USA TODAY, 14 AUGUST, 1996

STUDENT VOICES

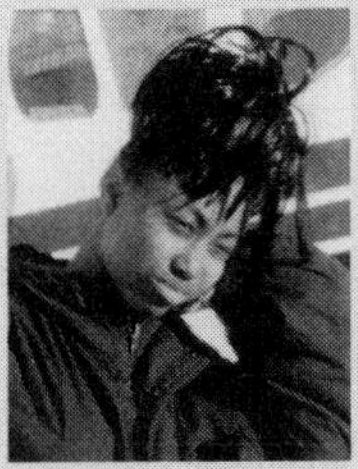

Flying prepares you for life! You don't have to be afraid of anything. Whatever you want to do, you can accomplish it.

TAKELA BUTLER
BALTIMORE, MD

STUDENT VOICES

I felt scared at first, but after we were flying for a while, I got the hang of it, and it was fun. I enjoyed looking down on the Potomac River, the houses looked like little monopoly buildings.

CRYSTAL HOLLOWAY
BALTIMORE, MD

A Balancing Act

Purpose
To find the center of gravity of an airplane.

Background
Your company is planning to build an airplane for the big Air Show. You've already talked with an experienced aircraft designer, and she had one piece of advice: "It all depends on the center of gravity. . .the plane won't fly correctly unless the center of gravity is in the right place."

But you're not sure what this *center of gravity* thing is, and how do you find it in an airplane? You've got to figure out a way to find the center of gravity of an airplane-shaped object. Maybe if you can find the center of gravity of a flat airplane, you may be able to use the same method with the air show model you are planning.

Materials
- meter stick
- cardboard
- scissors
- sheet of notebook or copier paper
- straight pin, thumb tack, or bent paper clip
- string
- several large washers (all the same size)

Procedure
Work in pairs to complete this activity.

Part 1
Examine a meter stick. Where do you think the stick will balance on your outstretched finger? Write your prediction in your log. Now try to actually balance the meter stick. Use your prediction as the starting point.

If the stick does not balance at that point, move it a little at a time until the meter stick balances perfectly. When it does, the center of gravity of the meter stick is directly above your finger.

Part 2
Look in books and magazines for pictures of airplanes viewed from the top. When you have found a good one to use as a model, sketch a top view of it on a piece of cardboard. Be sure the wings are the same size on both sides. Carefully cut out your airplane picture. Try to balance it. Use your finger or the eraser end of a pencil. When your plane cutout finally balances, draw a small circle around the balance point.

Part 3
The trouble with the center of gravity in a real airplane is that it doesn't stay put. You put the center of gravity to be in one place, then real people board the plane. Some are big and some are small. They don't even sit where you want them to. Before you know it, the center of gravity has moved.

What determines the new position of the center of gravity?

Fasten several washers to each of three strings. Hang two of the weighted strings on the meter stick somewhere between 0 and 49 cm. Try again to balance the stick/washer system on your finger. In your log record what happens. Try to find a position for the third weighted string so that the center of gravity of the entire system is at 50 cm. When your meter stick balances, make a drawing in your log of your balanced stick/washer system.

Part 4
Part 4 is the math part. For each weighted string, **multiply** its **distance** from the center of gravity **times** the **number of washers** on the string. The result represents the ***torque*** produced by the washers. Write these torque numbers next to the strings on your drawing. Add up the *torques* produced by the two weights on the 0 to 49 cm side of

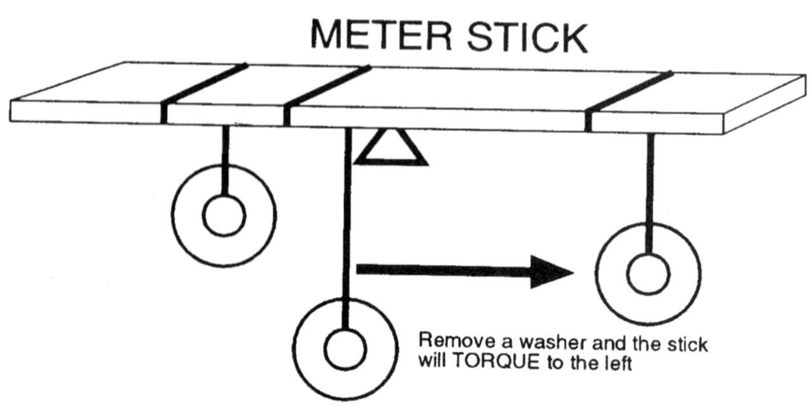

the stick. How does their sum compare to the *torque* produced by the washers on the other end?

***Torque* is the tendency for a system to rotate.** When you first added weights to the meter stick and tried to balance it, the meter stick tilted in the direction of the weights. It rotated around your finger! Think of a time when you and a friend played on a seesaw. What happened when one person decided to get off while the other was high off the ground?

Part 5

Now use a different method to find the center of gravity of the cardboard plane cutout. Push a pin through one edge of the plane and attach it to a bulletin board so the cardboard swings freely from the pin. Hang a weighted string on the pin. Make a mark where the string crosses the opposite edge of your airplane. Draw a straight line from the pin to the new mark. Change the position of the pin and repeat the above procedure. Then try a third pin position. The point of intersection of the three lines is the center of gravity of the airplane shape. Test this by balancing the plane on the eraser end of a pencil. If it doesn't balance, redo the procedure, checking the locations of the intersecting lines.

Part 6

Fold a paper airplane using a piece of notebook or copier paper. Devise a method to find its center of gravity. Remember, this plane is not flat, it's three-dimensional. Finding its center of gravity is more complicated than it was with the flat cardboard plane.

Conclusion

Make a display showing your cardboard cutout, and your paper airplane. Add other diagrams if they will help you explain the concept of center of gravity to others.

Also include your answer to this problem:

You're the Operations Manager for a small commuter airline. You are loading a flight to a nearby city. The plane can carry 20 passengers whose average weight is 150 pounds.

Ten people have shown up for the flight. They all have luggage, and one passenger is pushing a cart containing an automobile engine weighing over 1000 pounds. The luggage is stored under the passenger compartment. How would you assign seats to the 10 people on the flight, and how would you arrange the engine and the other luggage? Explain your answers. A diagram may be helpful.

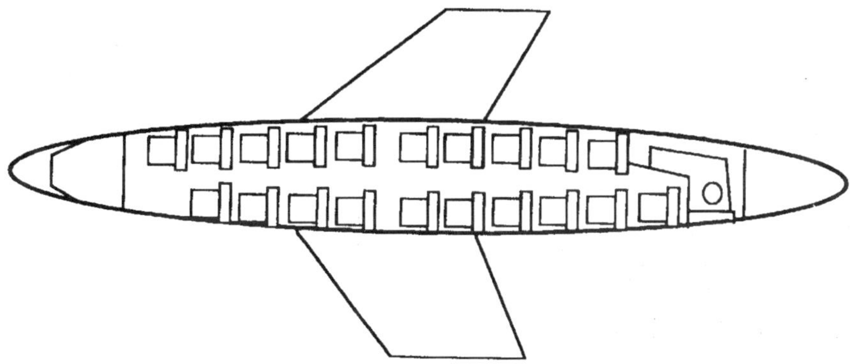

DISCOVERY FILE

Aviation Firsts: Milestones in the History of Flight

c. 1490	Leonardo da Vinci sketches designs for human-powered helicopter, flying machine, and parachute
1783	Montgolfier brothers launch hot-air balloons carrying animals and later, people
1849	Sir George Cayley's glider carries a boy a short distance
1891	Otto Lilienthal builds and flies the first practical glider
1903	Wright brothers achieve first true powered flight in their *Wright Flyer*
1914	World War I (1914–1918): first aerial combat in wartime
1918	first regular airmail service
1923	first nonstop transcontinental flight
1924	first round-the-world flight
1927	Charles Lindbergh is the first person to solo across the Atlantic in the *Spirit of St. Louis*
1932	Amelia Earhart is first woman to fly solo across the Atlantic
1933	Boeing 247 is first modern passenger airliner
1937	Frank Whittle's first jet engine is tested
1939	Igor Sikorsky designs and flies single rotor helicopter, first jet plane is flown in Germany, World War II (1939–1945): airplane becomes major military weapon
1947	Charles Yeager breaks sound barrier in X-1 rocket plane
1958	jet airliners begin commercial flights in United States.
1969	astronauts walk on the moon
1976	supersonic *Concorde* begins carrying passengers
1977	*Gossamer Condor*, Paul MacCready's first human-powered aircraft, flies $7\frac{1}{2}$ minutes
1979	Bryan Allen pedals Paul MacCready's *Gossamer Albatross* across English Channel
1981	first reusable manned space vehicle—the space shuttle—is launched
1986	*Voyager* circles Earth in nine days without refueling
1995	solar-powered *Pathfinder* flies higher than 50,000 feet

How aircraft are maintained and repaired

All planes require periodic heavy maintenance. But now that the domestic jet fleet is the oldest it's been since jet service started about 35 years ago, repairs and refurbishments are becoming more routine, more complex and more expensive. And with a plane, particularly an aging one, much of what is replaced or rebuilt is mandated by the Federal Aviation Administration. USAir calls the heaviest of its maintenance jobs a "Q" check, which for a basic McDonnell Douglas DC-9 comes every 10,500 hours of flying time or about every four years. It involves about 2,000 separate procedures which take at least 20 days and cost more than $2 million.

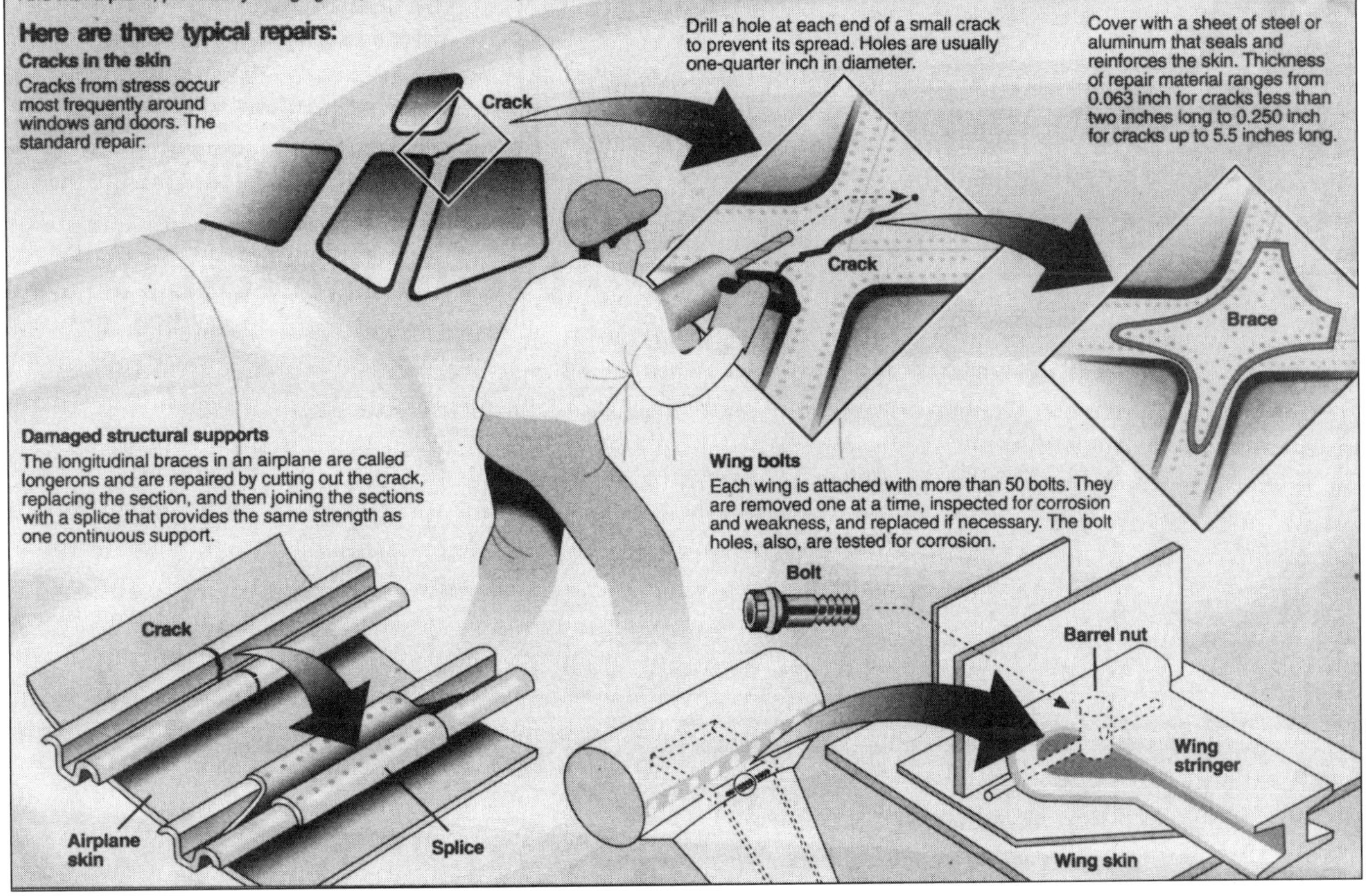

USA TODAY, 5 JULY, 1996

Leonardo's Flying Machine

Leonardo da Vinci (1452–1519)—a genius as painter, scientist, inventor, engineer, and sculptor—can truly be called a *Renaissance Man.* In his plans and drawings we can see the ideas for some modern machines and inventions. However, it is very unlikely that he actually influenced modern inventors. Perhaps to protect his ideas, Leonardo wrote in a code called *mirror writing,* and after his death his sketches and notebooks were lost for centuries.

In his thirties, Leonardo began to study the flight of birds and make detailed sketches of his observations. He drew designs for a pedal-powered flying machine, a parachute, a helicopter, and even landing gear.

His pedal-powered machine, which he called an *ornithopter* (from two Greek words meaning *bird* and *wing*), used flapping wings. Made of wood, metal, and feathers, a model of the original design weighed over 600 pounds. It was far too heavy to fly.

Leonardo never fully understood how birds fly. Despite many hours of studying their bones and muscles, he concluded that birds flap their wings down and back in order to fly. He was wrong. He also did not fully grasp the concept of *lift,* a theory that would be left to others to explore and define. His theories for bird flight were shown to be impossible in 1685 by biologist and engineer Giovanni Borelli.

Leonardo never realized his dream of human-powered flight for several reasons. He based his designs on the flapping wings of birds. He did not realize that human muscles are not strong enough to flap wings that are big enough. He also did not have the technology or an understanding of aerodynamics. Despite these drawbacks, his designs speak to us from 500 years ago.

Leonardo's sketch for a parachute looks amazingly like a modern-day one. And his helicopter-like machine, while too heavy to fly and lacking the power to lift off the ground, employed the principle of a vertical screw.

Leonardo was right about the possibility of human powered flight. Centuries later, the human-powered *Gossamer Albatross* (weighing about 200 pounds) flew across the English Channel. Made of piano wire, cardboard, aluminum, and plastic—materials unknown in Leonardo's time and considerably lighter—this pedal-powered machine did fly.

Though Leonardo's machines were never built and never flew, they tell a story of a remarkable mind. He was the first to make a scientific attempt to invent a flying machine.

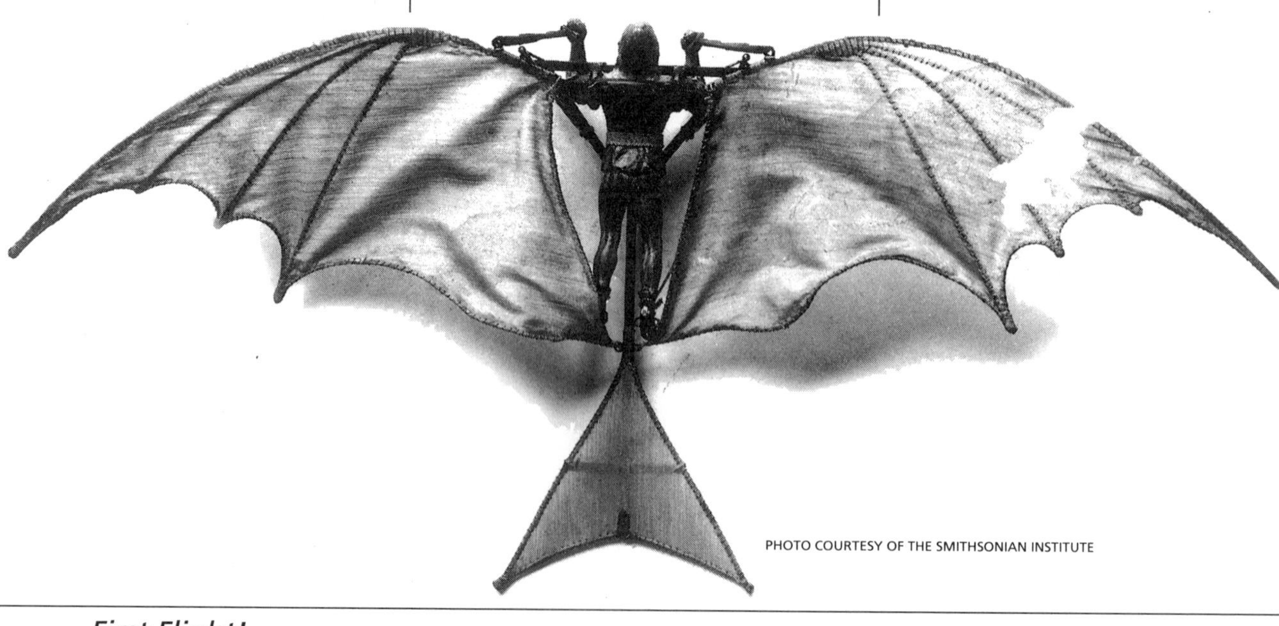

PHOTO COURTESY OF THE SMITHSONIAN INSTITUTE

DISCOVERY FILE

Natural-Born Fliers

The flight of birds inspired Leonardo da Vinci and many other inventors of flying machines. But these early inventors lacked an understanding of the structural differences between birds and humans. They also lacked an understanding of the principles of aerodynamics—*lift* and *gravity, thrust* and *drag.* Because of their lack of knowledge, early inventors usually modeled their designs on the flapping wings of birds.

Many early flying contraptions were based on the idea that if flapping wings enabled birds to fly, then flapping wings were needed for people to fly. These inventors had not studied anatomy. They didn't realize that birds' bodies are designed for flying. Even a flightless bird like the penguin "flies" through the water. Birds have mostly hollow bones and lightweight skeletons. They also have large muscles attached to their chests and backs in order to flap their wings.

Human chest and back muscles are too weak to flap wings big enough to lift a person.

Some of the early would-be human flyers built mechanical wings and attached them to their bodies. These "tower jumpers," as they were called, leaped from high places, expecting to soar into the air. They were brave but foolish people. All of them failed.

When the principles of aerodynamics were understood, human flight became possible. Some inventors continued using the flapping wing design into the 20th century, but eventually everyone got the message. Humans are different from birds. We need machines to fly.

Although, some soaring birds, like the albatross and condor, glide on rising air currents or thermals to save energy. Most of the over-9,000 species of birds in the world fly.

Wing shape and size varies among birds, and determines the way they fly, as well as their lifestyle. An eagle has very broad, strong wings and swoops down to pick up its prey. The wings of smaller birds show they are built for flying quickly for long periods of time.

The upper surface of a bird wing is curved; the lower surface is flat. Lift is produced by the difference in air pressure over and under the wing when the bird is in flight.

After birds take off, they can fold their feet back like a plane's retractable landing gear; they can also bring their feet forward to land.

Different kinds of feathers on a bird each serve a different purpose. The longest ones push the bird forward. Feathers close to the wing tip help the bird turn. Tail feathers act as a rudder to help the bird steer or brake. Leonardo was so sure that he understood the function of a bird's wing tip that he designed elaborate pulleys and hinges for clenching the tips of wings on his flying machine. He was mistaken about how a bird's wings really work, but he was right about one thing. Wings hold the key to flight.

The hummingbird, the smallest species of bird, weighs only two to twenty grams. It has the unique abilities to hover and to fly backward. The wings of a hummingbird beat 80 times a second.

Many of the over-750,000 species of insects also fly. Airborne insects have flat wings connected to the thorax, or central segment of their bodies. A tiny insect like a mosquito can flap its wings over 500 times every second. The common housefly beats its wings 200 times a second. Flapping the wings up and down uses a great deal of energy. It's worth it though. The speed compensates for the lack of lifting power. The effect of the flapping wings is said to be the same as a propeller going around and around. The stream of air directed down and backward sends the insect up and forward.

Among insects, the dragonfly is a ace flier. Even the U.S. Air Force, which has tested dragonflies in wind tunnels, cannot explain their aerial maneuvers.

Only one species of mammals is a true flyer—the bat. In fact, bats have inspired some modern flying machines. Flying birds, insects, and bats are natural fliers with many adaptations that enable them to take to the air.

On the Job

Chief Aerospace Engineer

Dave Pilkington
Vice President, Engineering
Aviat Aircraft

There's an old saying in aviation, "Pick up a part that is supposed to go on the airplane and throw it up in the air. If it falls to the ground, it's too heavy to put on the airplane." You need to think about that one when you design aircraft.

I've been interested in airplanes ever since I can remember. I'd always wanted to be a pilot, but it wasn't until almost the end of high school I even knew there was such a thing as an aerospace engineer. I studied physics and the logical conclusion was, I could be a physicist. But it's more exciting to fly and design airplanes. In those days you needed perfect vision to get a commercial pilot's license. So I decided to go to university in aeronautical engineering, when I also learned to fly.

Right now, I'm on a three-year working visa and am presently the vice-president of engineering for Aviat Aircraft in Afton, Wyoming. Aviat builds two kinds of aircraft, an aerobatics trainer with fabric-covered wooden wings, and a two-seater bush plane. I saw this job advertised when I was in Australia, applied for it, and now here I am.

I'm the only engineer here, so I do all the engineering. An aerospace engineer at a large aircraft manufacturer would specialize in one part of the airplane. But in a small company, you have the whole plane to deal with—from the electrical system, to the engine, to the structure.

For about 20 years, I've flown planes built by my company. I fly in an Australian aerobatics group. It's unusual to fly and be an engineer, but it's a definite advantage when testing or demonstrating aircraft to customers. I'd recommend that someone who wants to get involved in the design side of aviation learn to fly.

Designing aircraft is a team effort. The team you are working on will include a draftsperson, R&D personnel, and another engineer who does a bit of troubleshooting, some drawing, and some production work.

The starting point in designing an aircraft is to determine the objective. We might even get some input from potential customers about what they want.

Early in the design process, we analyze the structure and make sure it's strong enough. Sometimes we can do that analysis by computer. It's cheaper and faster. But some components are too hard to analyze on computer. It's more effective to test them. We might build a component and load sandbags on it to see if it's strong enough.

Next comes the flight tests. We need to check for ourselves that each aircraft does the job we had intended for it. We need to prove that it meets government regulations for flight worthiness. That might mean such things as testing for carbon dioxide inside the airplane. Fire hazards are a big concern. We need to do flying tests on materials used inside the plane to make sure they are not too flammable. We also need to look at crash worthiness.

An important function of the aerospace engineer is to serve on the material review board. If something is not done right on the production line, it's expensive to scrap it and start again. Say you've got a wing nearly finished and someone drills a hole in the wrong place or drills the wrong size hole, then we go over and have a look at it and decide what to do. Do we say it's all right as it is, do we do a repair, or do we throw that bit away?

Besides designing, I also write reports about our designs for the FAA. We write flight manuals that have to be understood by people in different countries, so you need to be able to communicate and your English has to be fairly accurate. Instructions in one maintenance manual read, "Drain the propeller." The intent was to drain the oil from the propeller, but the person reading it said, "Well, I've got this propeller on the airplane, how do I drain the propeller from the airplane?"

If you want to design airplanes, start by reading aviation books and magazines. Try to learn from other people's mistakes. You don't have to reinvent the wheel. Just look at what other people have done.

The most important thing to consider is to build the structure light. Don't add anything that will add unnecessary weight. The aircraft should also be easy to repair or replace.

Unnecessary ounces add up fast. Our planes weigh about 1,200 pounds. If we can save 50 pounds, that's an extra two hours in the air without refueling. A coat of paint might weigh twenty pounds. If paint is applied too thick, it adds extra weight the plane can't accept. As an engineer, you have to deal with this problem. The control surfaces must balance perfectly. If the paint is too thick on one of the ailerons, we have to send it back to be stripped and done again.

Aerospace engineering is the most difficult of the engineering courses. You're going to need good marks in math, physics, English. You need English because you'll need to communicate with people. This is a very competitive field. When a big company has a project, it recruits a lot of people. When the project ends, they get rid of the people. Expect to move if you become an aerospace engineer.

STUDENT VOICES

When I get older I might own a plane, and this experience will help me be able to fly it.

If I were designing an airplane, I would save money and weight by leaving off most of the fancy things, and other things you don't need.

ERICA WILLIAMS
BALTIMORE, MD

STUDENT VOICES

I wanted to go flying, because when I grow up, I want to be a Navy pilot. I want to fly jets. My first flight felt like a roller coaster in the sky. The winds bounced us up and down. It gave me butterflies in my stomach.

If I were designing a plane, to save money and weight, I'd make it out of fiberglass.

LAZAROS STAVROU
BALTIMORE, MD

DISCOVERY FILE

What a Drag!

Drag is one of the four forces that acts on an airplane in flight. It is the one that opposes the forward motion of the plane. Many people think that drag is caused by friction, or rubbing, between the air and the airplane. This is not true!

Drag is actually caused by the airplane stirring up the air and creating *turbulence.* The more turbulence an airplane creates, the more drag that is produced.

If an airplane could slip through the air without creating turbulence there would be little drag. There would, however, be friction.

SCIENCE ACTIVITY

Out To Launch

Purpose
To explore the effects of structural changes on the flight of a paper airplane.

Background
Your engineering company got a request from a children's magazine. Their writers are preparing an article about how paper airplanes fly, and the editor wants to include instructions on how to make the airplanes turn, loop, fly straight and level, and land safely. That's your job!

You will conduct a series of experiments to explore the various factors in the design of a paper airplane that produce different moves. The editors want evidence that you have actually tested paper airplanes yourself. After that, you will write a memo stating your findings.

Materials
- paper airplane pattern
- sheets of paper
- paper clips
- tape
- stopwatch or watch with a second hand
- ruler or tape measure

Procedure
Work with one partner to complete this activity. Start by making a paper airplane. Use your own design or use the blackline master pattern your teacher gives you. If you prefer to use your own design, make sure it has wings. Make all folds very sharp by using the side of a pen or pencil to press down on each fold.

Now you are ready to begin experimenting. Use the method you learned in the previous activity to find the center of gravity of your paper airplane. Make a mark to show this point.

Rules to Consider
- The same person should make all launches in a set of trials.
- Practice the launch motion; try to make it the same each time. Launch in an open area without strong winds or drafts. Measure the distance from the launcher to the landing point.
- Keep a log of your results. In it, *briefly* describe or draw the flight path for each trial.
- Repeat the launch a few times and find the average flight distance. (Discuss how many launches is enough to give you a good average.)
- Be sure the plane looks the same before each launch. (In other words, repair any damage from landings or collisions. If damage to your first plane causes you to make another one, try to make it exactly the same as the first.)

When you are ready to modify your plane, remember to make it turn, loop, fly straight, and land safely. Change something about your plane that you predict will help it reach one of these goals. Consider changes in the wings' shape or adding weight to the plane. Make only one change at a time. After each change, launch the plane several times. Continue to record the each flight path. Calculate and record the average distance before you make a design change.

Your findings will be sent to the magazine editor in the form of a memo. Your teacher will have a sample memo for you to use. Your memo should be easy to read and well-organized. Remember, the editors of the magazine have no experience with airplanes. Keep your explanations simple. Be sure to include a labeled diagram of your paper airplane. Show its parts and its center of gravity.

Conclusion
Be sure to include the following points as you write your memo to the editor.

1. Describe the feature of your paper airplane that produced the straightest flight, the best right turn, the best left turn, the best climb, and the best dive.
2. If you used a paper clip, explain the effect it had on the flight of the airplane. Describe its position.
3. How did you decide on the number of launches for each trial? What are the benefits of doing a lot of launches? What are the problems with doing a lot of launches?
4. In a controlled experiment on paper airplanes, all launches in each set of trials should start exactly the same way. Comment on problems you had in making all launches the same. Were you able to solve these problems? Explain.

What Materials Should I Use?

In 1783, the Montgolfier brothers were the first to achieve a kind of flight with their lighter-than-air balloons made of paper and cloth, held together with buttons and stitches. Later, hot-air balloons used silk for their envelopes and wicker baskets for the gondola.

One hundred years ago, Otto Lilienthal was building gliders out of wood, cotton, canvas, and wire. A few years later, Wilbur and Orville Wright built their historic *Wright Flyer* out of ordinary materials too. They made the wings from ashwood covered with muslin; sprucewood was used to make bracing struts and the curved propellers. They also used bicycle chains and wire. The total cost of materials came to $15.

In less than a century, aircraft have undergone all kinds of transformations—in design, aerodynamics, function, technology, even materials. Lightweight synthetics and alloys have changed the world of aviation completely. Early aviators might recognize the shape of airplanes today but not the materials.

In the 1960s, new materials revived interest in hot-air ballooning. Envelopes of polyurethane-coated nylon, filled with hot air rising from propane heaters, allowed balloons to be made in all shapes. Some recreational balloonists who compete in distance events ride in aluminum capsules beneath their balloons, but wicker baskets are still popular. Wicker is strong, light, and flexes to absorb the shock of a landing.

The nylon, a synthetic fiber created in the 1930s, is also used in today's parachutes and parasails.

While Lilienthal's gliders resembled today's gliders, they used very different materials. Lightweight frames of metal tubes and cables have replaced the wood and canvas, and todays flexible wings are made of synthetic fabrics that are light, yet strong and tear-resistant. Aluminum alloys and carbon fibers have made modern hang gliding a popular sport.

As aircraft became more technologically advanced and began to fly higher and faster, the stresses of flight changed, too. Flying machines now serve many functions, from commercial to military. The wood and wires of the *Wright Flyer* and other early aircraft have been replaced by aluminum alloys, carbon fibers, and composites that can withstand the stresses of high-speed and high altitudes.

After the introduction of the jet engine, engineers searched for materials capable of withstanding high temperatures within jet engines and heating of the plane's surface caused by drag. Today's jumbo jets need a fuselage strong enough to withstand the stress of repeated pressurization and depressurization without cracking or springing leaks.

Airliners are made of millions of components, from giant titanium-blade fans to many miles of wires. As the demand for faster and cheaper airplanes grows, structural engineers will continue their search for materials to reduce the weight of the plane. An aluminum-lithium alloy used in some wing sections shows promise.

Engines are also the subject of research, as engineers look for materials to improve performance. One possibility is a composite made of metal and ceramics. Such an engine would be lighter, while producing the required thrust with less fuel.

Aerodynamic and economic requirements pose many challenges to the engineers and designers of the future. As materials change, so will aviation.

IN THE NEWS

U.S. to order rudder change on every 737

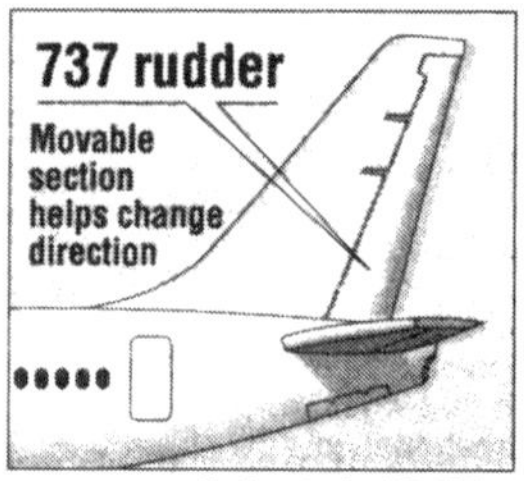

By Grant Jerding, USA TODAY

By Lori Sharn
and David Field
USA TODAY

The FAA will order Boeing to improve rudder control on the world's most widely flown jet, the Boeing 737.

Vice President Gore said Wednesday that Boeing will pay for most of the changes, part of an effort to prevent another unexplained crash.

The changes should eliminate the possibility that a rudder will move on its own, sending the jet out of control. The changes also give pilots more control if sharp rudder movements occur anyway.

"We want to ensure that the rudder moves only when the pilot wants it to," says acting FAA administrator Linda Daschle. The FAA will order the changes within days.

The order is not, both Boeing and the FAA stress, an admission that rudder malfunctions caused still-unexplained 737 crashes near Pittsburgh in 1994 and in Colorado Springs in 1991. Both jets suddenly rolled and plunged to the ground, killing all on board, 157 in all.

"This is a safe plane, and these steps will make a safe plane safer," Southwest Airlines' Kristie Kerr said.

About 2,700 Boeing 737s are flying worldwide, including 1,115 in U.S. fleets.

Last week the FAA ordered 737 pilots to get extra training in handling unexpected rolls.

Boeing says some modifications may not be completed until 2000 because parts will need to be made. Boeing and its subcontractors will pay for the new parts, up to $140 million. Airlines will provide labor.

USA TODAY, 16 JANUARY, 1997

IN THE NEWS

FAA gives grounded ATR the OK for takeoff

By Paul Hoversten
USA TODAY

The Federal Aviation Administration pronounced the controversial ATR turboprop fit to fly in icy weather Wednesday, a month after barring it from service where ice might occur.

But the agency issued guidelines on operating the ATR, ordered new de-icing detection equipment for the planes and will require new training for pilots and dispatchers.

"I would get on and fly it," said FAA chief David Hinson, who added U.S. airlines might restore ATR service within a week. "This is a very good airplane. It is perfectly safe if it's flown in accordance with the new procedures."

When the planes were banned from cold-weather routes, commuter airline schedules were thrown into chaos until other types of aircraft were substituted.

The restrictions on the 48-seat ATR 42 and 69-seat ATR 72 came after the Oct. 31 crash in Roselawn, Ind., of an ATR 72 that killed 68 people. Ice buildup on the wings was suspected to have caused an abrupt roll and loss of control by the pilots.

Wednesday's action does not address the cause of that crash, which the National Transportation Safety Board is still investigating. "The last thing I want to do is give you the impression we have solved the Roselawn crash," said Anthony Broderick, head of FAA regulation.

But pilots now are restricted from moving the wing flaps, which provide lift, when the plane is flying in icy conditions — whenever moisture is visible and the temperature is below 40 degrees F.

Randolph Babbitt, president of the Air Line Pilots Association, called the ATR safe when flown under the new rules.

But some pilots and passengers remained skeptical.

"This is a whitewash," said pilot Steve Fredrick, who was suspended from American Eagle after speaking out on concerns about the safety of ATRs early last month. "They're playing Russian roulette with the statistics and there's still a bullet in the chamber. I still wouldn't get on the doggone thing until they prove it's safe."

Said Stacy Lennard, a Florida hairstylist in transit at Chicago's O'Hare International Airport: "I still don't want to get on one. It's so small it's like a closet with wings."

Investigators in France and the U.S. used wind tunnels, supercomputers and a U.S. Air Force tanker spraying midair droplets to see how the ATR performed in icy conditions.

They found ice could form in unprotected areas of the wing and that wing flap movement could produce a severe roll and possible loss of control.

Avion de Transport Regional, the French-Italian manufacturer, within a week will put ice detection sensors — now standard on 72s — on ATR 42s.

The manufacturer also will install by June 1 a larger de-icing boot to cover twice as much wing space — 16% — as the previous version. The boot is a rubberized tube that inflates to knock ice off the wings.

The FAA action "comes at the end of extraordinary scrutiny," said Alain Brodin, president of ATR Marketing Inc., Chantilly, Va. "No other aircraft, commercial or military, has ever had this kind of testing . . . and we came out of that inspection with flying colors."

About 400 ATRs have been flying worldwide since 1985.

Contributing: K.V. Johnson

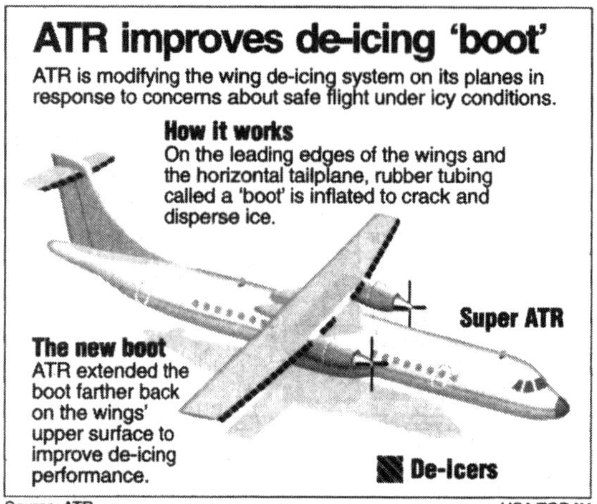

Source: ATR USA TODAY

USA TODAY, 12 JANUARY, 1995

The Wright Stuff

PHOTO COURTESY OF THE SMITHSONIAN INSTITUTE

Orville and Wilbur Wright returned to Kitty Hawk in the winter of 1901 with a new glider. But quickly became discouraged. Insects and birds were the only things flying at Kitty Hawk. After a series of crashes, the brothers gave up and returned to Dayton. Wilbur and Orville began to think that the lift tables they had been using could be wrong. They decided to design new wing shapes, and collect their own data. They built small models of different airfoils and tested them in a homemade wind tunnel. With the data from these tests they created new, more accurate, tables of lift.

Besides lift, control was a major problem for early aviators. To control their glider, Orville and Wilbur had already invented a technique they called "wing-warping."

In the Wright brothers' glider, the pilot would lie facedown on the lower of two wings. From that position he would steer. A rudder controlled yaw, and wing-warping allowed the glider roll—to bank, or tilt, into a turn. With wing-warping, when the right wing twisted up, the left wing twisted down. It worked! Their glider now was controllable.

Finally, the Wright brothers were ready to try again. They took their new glider to Kitty Hawk. They began to set flight distance records.

By 1903, Orville and Wilbur had mastered lift and control. But how could they power their aircraft? A steam engine—the main source of power in the 19th century—was too heavy. So were the gasoline-powered engines used in automobiles. The Wright brothers had no choice. They designed and built a 12-horsepower gasoline engine to power their *Wright Flyer*. Their engine was smaller, and lighter-weight than anything else available. With two propellers fashioned from sprucewood, the brothers were truly ready to fly.

December 14th, 1903—six days after Langley's humiliation in the Potomac—the brothers flipped a coin to see who would be the first to fly. Wilbur won. His newly-powered glider flew $3\frac{1}{2}$ seconds before it nosed into the sand.

Three days later, after making repairs, they were ready to try again. On the beach at 10:35 A.M. on that cold morning near Kitty Hawk, North Carolina, it was Orville's turn. Wilbur pulled down hard on one of the propellers. The engine started. The 605-pound flying machine accelerated down the track and rose into the air. This time, it remained airborne for a full 12 seconds. It actually flew 120 feet. There were four flights in all that day. The longest was 859 feet and lasted 59 seconds.

Although powered flight had finally been achieved, very few people paid attention. Only a handful of newspapers reported the story. It wasn't until the end of 1905, that the press finally began to notice the Wright brothers' experiments. After years with little attention from the press, in 1905 Orville and Wilbur were forced to stop flying to keep their ideas from reporters.

But in spite of press coverage of their flying successes, the Langley disaster made United States government officials very skeptical. The frustrated brothers decided to take their flying machines on the road. Wilbur headed to Europe, Orville to sites across America.

Meanwhile, the French, believing that they would be the first to fly, thought the Wright brothers' claims were lies. But, in 1908, when Wilbur demonstrated that their machine could really fly, the people of Europe went wild. Orville and Wilbur become celebrities, and the U.S. military at last was interested.

Discovery File

Control Surfaces

Unlike cars, which can only be steered right or left, birds and airplanes move in three dimensions. In airplanes this is achieved by changing the position of the plane's control surfaces. Birds have built-in control surfaces. Their feather-covered wings and tail control their flight. Airplanes have a *rudder, elevators,* and *ailerons* to control their movement through the air.

These movable control surfaces actually change the shape of an airplane. They can make an airplane either more or less streamlined. Control surfaces also create more or less lift as needed to make turns, banks, climbs, glides, and dives.

Cables or hydraulic lines run from the pedals or control stick to the control surfaces on most airplanes. When a pilot moves the stick or pedals, a mechanical connection moves the control surfaces. (In the Airbus 320 series, a "fly-by-wire" system in which computers send electrical signals to motors is used. The motors move the control surfaces.) By either method, changing the position of the control surfaces, causes movements called yawing, pitching, or rolling.

The **elevator** on the rear edge of the tailplane changes the pitch and makes the plane go up or down. Pointing the plane up increases lift. But it's not that simple. If the plane climbs at too steep an angle, it loses speed. Less speed means less lift, and too little lift can cause a stall.

The **rudder,** at the back of the tail fin, makes the plane point left or right, in what is called yawing. (In the *Wright Flyer* and other early aircraft, the rudder and elevator were both mounted on the front of the aircraft.)

The rudder alone does not provide enough control to make a turn. To really make an airplane turn, the plane has to tilt, or bank, at the same time it is yawing. In the Flyer, the Wright brothers introduced an innovation they called "wing-warping" (bending or twisting). In this technique, they used wires connected to the ends of the wings.

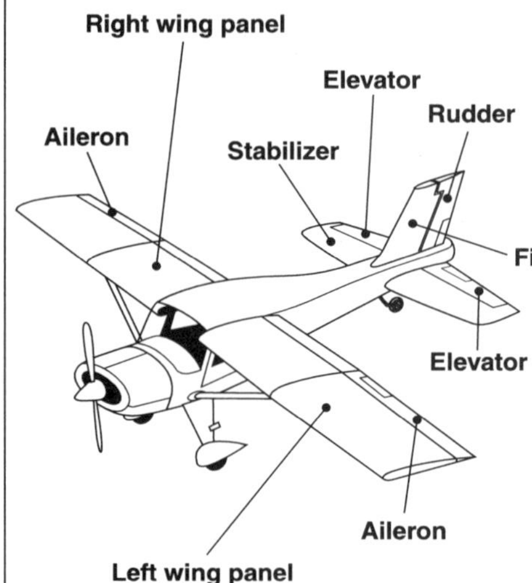

The control surfaces

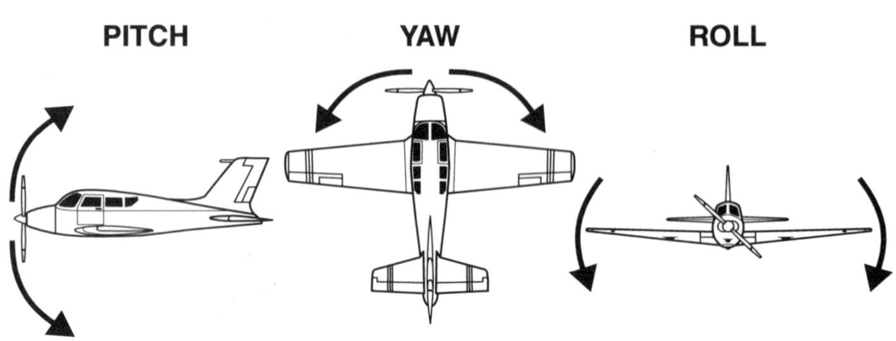

Pulling the wires twisted the wings, causing the plane to roll. Warping and twisting was eventually replaced by ailerons.

Ailerons are flaps on the rear edges of stiffer wings. Moving the ailerons up and down also causes the plane to roll. Other flaps and spoilers on the trailing edge of the wings are used when a plane takes off—for extra lift, and when it lands—for braking.

Flaps are used on most planes. Some ultralight and experimental aircraft have enough lift that they don't need flaps. By contrast, a 400-ton plane moving at relatively low speeds during takeoff and landing needs the additional lift provided by flaps.

A pilot uses a control stick and pedals to adjust the ailerons, elevators, and rudder. It takes a great deal of coordination and concentration to make the control surfaces work together.

SCIENCE ACTIVITY

Puppet Plane

Purpose

To analyze the forces that affect an airplane in flight.

Background

Your engineering firm bought time on the wind tunnel at a nearby university. Now you can actually test possible aircraft designs. You are especially concerned about how changes in the plane's pitch will affect lift and drag

Materials

- small balsa-wood glider
- electric fan
- thin string or thread
- 10 cm × 10 cm block of wood or stiff cardboard (or short dowel rods lashed with string or tape to make a + shape)

Procedure

Work in small groups to assemble a balsa glider according to instructions on the package. Find a way to position the finished glider in front of an electric fan. The glider must be free to move around in the wind without flying away. Suspending your glider from four strings, like a puppet, is one method that works well.

Start the experiment with the glider level and its nose pointed forward into the wind. Turn on the fan and record observations in your log. How is the glider being pushed or pulled by the wind?

Now change the *pitch* so that the nose is pointing slightly more or less upward. Test several different pitches. How does the glider react to changes in pitch?

Now change the wing position so that the center of gravity moves forward or back. How does the glider react to changes in its center of gravity? (For each center of gravity you try, test each of the pitch angles you tested above. Make only one center-of gravity change at a time. Record the effect that each change makes upon the actions of the glider. You may want to do some additional trials at different fan speeds.

This is your change to test control surfaces and design features you plan to use in your final airplane design. If there is anything else you decide to change, make those changes one at a time, too. Test all structural changes in each position or pitch used above. Organize your observations and findings into a fax memo to send to your company president. Use sketches to show how your plane responded to the various wind conditions.

Conclusion

When you prepare the fax memo to send to your company's president, be sure to report your findings and describe how the things you learned in the wind tests will be used in your final design.

Consider the following questions as you prepare your fax:

1. When the glider had zero pitch, it was level in the air stream, what evidence did you see for an upward force or *lift?* What evidence did you see for a backward force or *drag?* As you pitched the nose up, how did lift and drag forces change?
2. When you moved the center of gravity toward the front of the glider, what effect did that seem to have on lift and drag?
3. What design features did you test and how did they affect lift and drag?
4. What control surfaces did you test and how did they affect the motion of the glider?
5. Which of the features in your design will require a longer runway for takeoff?
6. Which of the features will require a shorter runway?
7. A few minutes before landing, an airline pilot lowers the flaps. Flaps are large panels on the rear edge of each wing that are lowered to cause the shape of the wing to curve downward. What effect does this have on lift and drag? Will you use flaps on your airplane design? Refer to your findings to defend your decision.

Extension

Before entering your plane in the big Air Show, use the puppet rig and electric fan to conduct flight tests and make final adjustments without risking your plane or its crew.

IN THE NEWS

In Alaska, crashes don't deter fliers

By Maria Goodavage
USA TODAY

JUNEAU, Alaska — Planes and helicopters buzz like mosquitoes, lifting tourists to once-in-a-lifetime glimpses of glaciers, forests and mountains.

Aerial sightseeing is booming business here. And a recent string of small-plane crashes, including a sightseeing flight last week, is not scaring away thrill-seekers.

"Now we'll just have to keep our fingers slightly crossed, but it's not going to deter us a bit," says Jack Maver of Melbourne, Australia, about to board a plane from a dock next to his cruise ship in Juneau.

Five crashes in 23 days have killed 20 people in the state. The latest, on July 7 near Haines in the southeast panhandle, killed six people on board a sightseeing flight. The crash occurred shortly after the pilot apparently turned the plane to look at a bear.

The other accidents, from central Alaska to the southwest, involved:

▶ A private float plane.

▶ A charter plane returning from a fishing trip.

▶ A private plane carrying a group from Ohio.

▶ A midair collision between a private plane and a plane owned by a fishing lodge.

"To have accidents of this nature, in five different areas, is highly unusual for us," says Dick Gordon of the Federal Aviation Administration.

Flying is an integral part of life in Alaska, where communities are separated by water, mountains and vast stretches of roadless tundra. Planes deliver mail and supplies, take people to work, even take some children to schools and sporting events.

> "Planes in Alaska are like taxi cabs in New York. Everyone needs them and everyone takes them."
>
> — **Michael O'Daniel, pilot**

There are nearly 10,000 aircraft in Alaska, one for every 59 residents and 14 times as many per capita as the rest of the USA. Lake Hood in Anchorage is the busiest seaplane base in the world.

"Planes in Alaska are like taxicabs in New York. Everyone needs them and everyone takes them," says Michael O'Daniel, a pilot for Skagway Air Service.

The spate of crashes came on the heels of two federal calls for tougher rules for pilots on tourism-related flights:

▶ The National Transportation Safety Board in May urged that hunting and fishing guides who fly clients in Alaska follow the same rules as on-demand charter flights. Now, such guides are only required to be licensed private pilots.

The board studied 29 accidents involving lodges or guides during a two-year period, and found most resulted from poor pilot judgment.

Gordon says the FAA already is working on changes for hunting and fishing guides.

Alaska's aviation accident toll

Ten aviation accidents have killed 26 people this year in Alaska. The average for the first seven months of the past five years is nine fatal crashes and 18 deaths. Fatal aviation accidents and fatalities for Alaska each year:

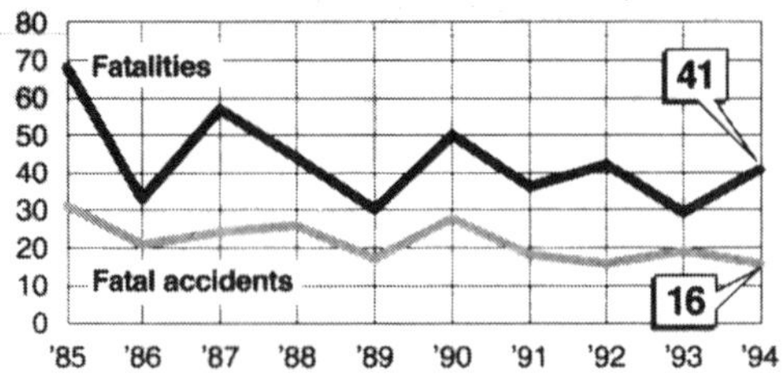

Fatal accident rates

The average fatal aviation accident rates[1] for Alaska, compared with those in the rest of the USA in 1990-94: (Rates are per 100,000 flight hours.)

	General aviation	Air taxi[2]	Commuters
Alaska	1.735	1.525	.547
Rest of USA	1.756	1.136	.187

1 – There were no fatal crashes of major airlines in Alaska during this time
2 – Includes charters and most sightseeing flights

Sources: Federal Aviation Administration; National Transportation Safety Board

By Genevieve Lynn, USA TODAY

▶ The NTSB in June also called for national standards by the end of the year for the air tour industry. The safety board investigated 139 air tour accidents between 1988 and April 1, including 16 in Alaska, that killed 117 people.

Flying can be more hazardous here because of the difficulties of flying around mountains and the many off-airport landings on lakes, sandbars and remote roads.

"It takes a lot more experience and talent to fly in Alaska," says Gordon. "There's a vast difference in how an airplane has to be operated."

Safety officials have worked for years to discourage "bush pilot syndrome," an attitude that it's OK to take risks.

"Fifteen years ago, there was a lot of pressure on some pilots. They were told, 'You will fly or we'll find someone else to fly.' So they went up even if they felt the conditions weren't right," says Marcel Shubert, a pilot for Era Helicopters. "It's not like that so much today. The disreputable firms have a way of going out of business."

More than 200,000 people are expected to take aerial sightseeing tours between May and September in Alaska. Skies are so congested near some parks that the operators have agreed to fly certain routes so they won't run into each other.

Skagway Air pilot Neil Gary says there's nothing worse than when a plane goes down.

"All it takes is a moment's lapse," he says.

"In the end, it all comes down to judgment, and you can't regulate judgment."

Contributing: Lori Sharn

USA TODAY, 14 JULY, 1995

Discovery File

Four Forces in Flight

When forces push and pull on things they can cause changes in motion. When we think about flight, our minds naturally focus on the force called *lift*—the force that holds the plane up in the air. But lift is only one of the forces that acts on a powered aircraft in flight. Three other forces are also important.

Lift: an upward force acting on the craft, produced by the downward deflection of air by the wings

Gravity: the downward pull of Earth's gravity on the weight or mass of the craft

Drag: resistance to forward movement, caused by turbulence and the work done in pushing the air out of the way

Thrust: force that pushes the craft forward through the air

One reason da Vinci's inventions never flew is that he—and other inventors in earlier centuries—lacked a complete understanding of these forces. If earlier people understood the forces affecting flight, they might have taken off, and the Wright brothers might have stayed in their bicycle business.

The four forces of flight—lift, gravity, drag and thrust—act at the same time. More lift than gravity and the plane will climb. Too much lift and the plane may climb too fast, lose speed, and stall. Less lift than gravity and the plane drops. If lift is very small, a steep dive and crash can result. The challenge of flying is trying to get just the right balance between pairs of opposing forces: lift and gravity, thrust and drag.

Lift is caused by something called *attack angle*. The wings of a plane in level flight are always tilted slightly upward. The leading edge is slightly higher than the trailing edge.

The special curved shape of an airplane's wings also contributes to lift. The attack angle and the curved upper surface of the wing cause air flowing across the top of the wing to become compressed. Compression of air above the wing causes the air to move faster than air flowing beneath. The faster flowing air exerts less pressure on the upper surface of the wing. Slower-moving air beneath exerts greater pressure. It pushes up on the wing. The faster the plane moves, the greater the lift. This phenomenon has a name—Bernoulli's principle.

The force opposing lift is gravity, or weight. It results from the pull of Earth's mass on the mass of the airplane—and the pull of the mass of the airplane on the mass of the Earth. The greater the mass of the aircraft, the more that gravity will pull it down, and the more lift required to get the plane off the ground. Bigger, heavier planes need bigger wings.

Thrust is the force that pushes a plane forward. Thrust is created by propellers or by jet engines.

Lift only occurs when a plane is moving and air is moving rapidly over and under the wing surfaces. Thrust is needed to give an airplane enough speed to overcome another force, called drag.

Just as lift is opposed by gravity, thrust is opposed by drag. Drag—the force that pushes against forward movement of the plane—occurs only when an aircraft is moving through the

Angle of Attack

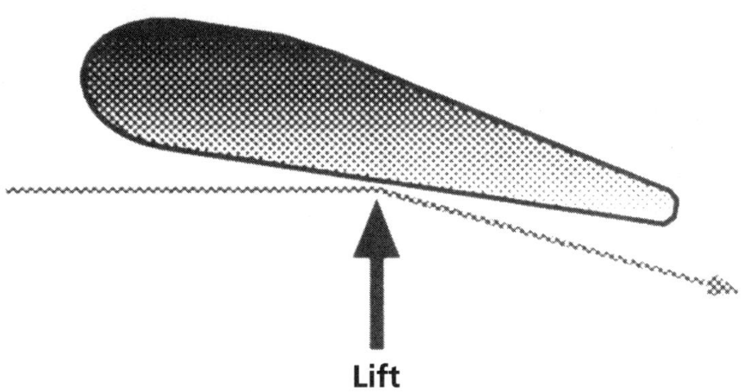

air and meets resistance. The smallest bumps on the surface of aircraft can disturb the smooth flow of air and add to drag.

The faster a plane moves the greater the resistance to movement. The greater the drag, the more thrust required to keep a plane moving. Because of drag, airplane designers are very concerned about making the most streamlined shape possible. With less drag, a plane can fly faster or need less thrust. Less thrust means less fuel. Less fuel means lower airfares or higher profits for the airlines.

Wing shape and attack angle are critical factors in drag. When Sir George Cayley started flying his gliders in the early 1800s, he observed that they were being held back by disturbances in the air. His straight wings created too much turbulence, or drag, that kept the glider from moving forward. Cayley solved the problem of drag by giving his wings a curved shape, over which air flowed smoothly.

Overall shape is also important when it comes to drag. The triangular shape of the space shuttle keeps drag low—especially important when the shuttle re-enters the atmosphere at very high speeds.

When an airplane needs to slow down, more drag is needed. Drag can be increased by raising flaps to increase the turbulence.

The same forces described here are at work on all kinds of aircraft, from hang gliders to supersonic jets. But they don't all apply to craft operating in space. Conditions outside of Earth's atmosphere are not the same. Can you figure out which forces are missing when rockets and spacecraft are operating in deep space?

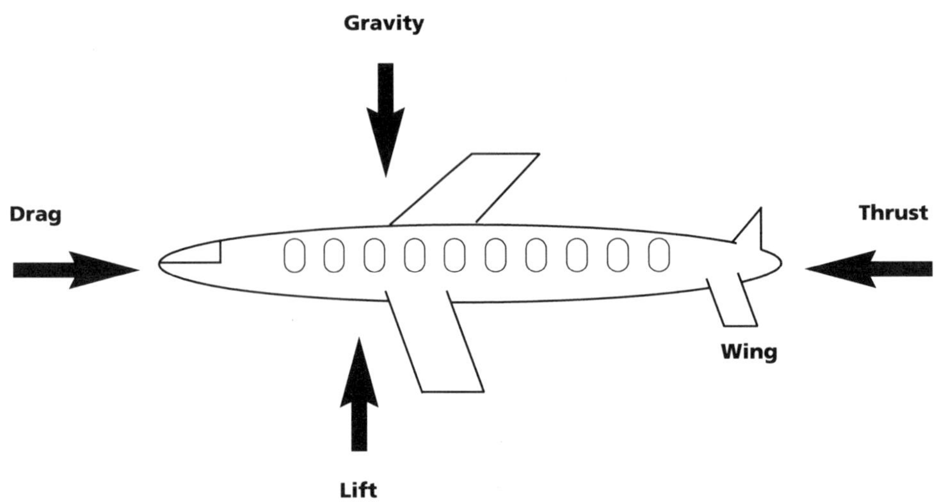

Discovery File

Bernoulli's Famous Principle

Who was Bernoulli and why was a whole principle named after him?

Dutch-born Swiss mathematician and physicist, Daniel Bernoulli (1700–1782) was from a well-known family of scientists. Both his father and uncle were famous mathematicians. Although Bernoulli studied philosophy and logic, mechanics and mathematics were his favorite subjects and the ones he had the most interest in investigating.

Daniel Bernoulli became famous for discovering principles in the field of *hydrodynamics* (also called *fluid mechanics*). In fact, he is credited with developing the science of hydrodynamics.

Bernoulli was the first person to state the relationship between pressure and speed (velocity) of moving fluids. (Fluids include gases and liquids.) Simply stated, Bernoulli's principle says that the faster a fluid flows, the lower the pressure it exerts.

An airplane's wings are shaped to take advantage of Bernoulli's principle. Having curved upper surfaces and flat bottom surfaces—a shape called an *airfoil*—causes the air passing over the top of the wing to travel faster *because it is compressed.* According to Bernoulli, the pressure of the air flowing faster over the wing is lower than the pressure of the air passing more slowly under the wing. The difference in pressure pushes the wing up and produces *lift.*

Bernoulli was right, but there is a problem with this explanation. It implies that shape alone accounts for lift, and that upside-down flight is impossible. Yet upside-down flight is far from impossible; it is common in all air shows. Also many wings do not have flat bottoms or unequal paths for the air passing over and under them. The thin cloth wings of the *Wright Flyer* are a good example.

Don't blame Bernoulli though. Although Bernoulli's water-based theory applies to other fluids like air, he never claimed that shape alone would produce a pressure difference great enough to lift a 400-ton airplane. (Remember, Bernoulli lived long before airplanes were even invented.)

Lift actually comes from a combination of the wing's shape and something called its *angle of attack.* Shape and the angle of attack combine to cause the air flowing over the wing to become compressed. It's the compression that speeds up the air. The result is the lowered pressure above the wing that Bernoulli predicted.

The shape of the wing is critical for another reason though. A straight wing creates a lot of turbulence. A curved wing has less turbulence and slips through the air with less resistance or drag.

Early inventors of would-be airplanes weren't successful because they lacked a complete understanding of aerodynamics. Had they understood more about forces that act on a plane in flight, people might have flown sooner.

Bernoulli's ideas can best be shown in water with a hydrofoil, which is also in the shape of an airfoil. A hydrofoil works even better to create lift because water is denser than air and gives more lift at lower speed. The name has been given to a kind of boat that can be said to "fly" through the water.

Student Voices

I was the first person this year to fly a mile high. I was flying straight, Mr. Taffel landed the plane. I didn't want to land. I was afraid I'd make a mistake and crash the plane.

Davon Bell
Baltimore, MD

On the Job

Customer Project Director

Robert Toy
Airbus Industrie

Our responsibility in the Customer Support Services Division is for the total in-service support of Airbus Industrie. I am a Chinese-American working for a company jointly owned by the French, British, Germans, and Spanish. My early days were spent in New York City where I was born, then in Oklahoma, and later in Texas, where I went to high school and attended the University of Texas. To be successful in today's aircraft industry—be it engineering, design, marketing, or customer support—you need to learn how to deal effectively in the international community.

My early background was in *avionics engineering* and *reliability analysis*, followed by program management and consulting. After four years in the U.S. Air Force, I lived and worked overseas on military electronics projects with American contractors. I've lived in Thailand, Germany, Poland, England, Iran, and Saudi Arabia, and traveled around the world. In 1992 I started working for Airbus Industrie. Today I live in Montaguit Sur Save, a tiny village north of Toulouse in southwestern France.

When I was growing up, I was interested in almost anything I could take apart to see how it worked. Unfortunately, putting things back together didn't always come as easy as the taking apart! But my single most interesting subject was people. What made people do some of the things they did? Why did different people react so differently to the same situation? For me this was a real challenge, I guess because I couldn't take them apart to find out how they worked!

As a kid—a minority, except I didn't feel like one—I could not understand why a person could behave so differently toward someone who was *different*, be it skin color, accent, or gender. Questioning this behavior had the greatest impact on my career choice and where I am today.

I have always been interested in airplanes and mechanical things. Although I stayed in the electronics field, I soon found myself analyzing failure and performance data trying to identify problem areas. This line of work fit perfectly with my personal passion of trying to figure out why and how things and people worked.

To me, mathematics and physics are the two most important sciences to study. It is difficult to imagine how important these subjects can be in any career. They teach us logic and discipline, something you will need to be able to use no matter what you do.

Using statistical analysis techniques to identify a problem and analyze a process (each step or action required to obtain a given response or reaction) is vital. For example: A marketing person for any product must be able to analyze the market, identify buying and spending habits, figure out what makes people choose one product over another, analyze the competition, and develop a marketing plan (process). An engineer must be able to analyze failures and malfunctions, identify a problem, design and fix it, and develop a modification plan (process).

What does someone in marketing need to think about? Know your customer! Does the customer need a 100-seat aircraft or a 300-seat aircraft? What range does he need? Where will she fly? How could you save money? Will the flights be long enough to need galleys? What impact does the customer's culture or values have on the product? For example, aircraft designed for Saudi Arabia have an electronic pointer in each cabin section that always points toward Mecca.

A good designer will have a basic knowledge of the customer's (airline) business, its setting, and its constraints. By ignoring these things, you can easily build a fantastic high-tech aircraft that is too small/large for the market; will not work properly in the climate; require expensive parts/highly skilled technicians, etc.

The aircraft manufacturing and support industry today is an international undertaking; the actual designing and building of aircraft spans the globe. The cockpit may be manufactured in one country, a part of the tail in another, the wings in another, and so on. The primary manufacturer collects various bits and pieces from sub-contractors and assembles them into an aircraft. Add to the aircraft shell the tens of thousands of bits and pieces ranging from nuts and bolts to state-of-the-art computers that control the aircraft and you now have a complete passenger aircraft.

I notice that part of your Task involves designing a sales brochure. When you are designing your brochure there are some additional things to keep in mind. Airplane manufacturers not only deliver aircraft, they also support the operation of their aircraft. This means providing the training, parts, documents, and other support to ensure the aircraft will fly safely, reliably, and profitably.

While today's aircraft design is largely driven by the airlines wanting to fly higher, faster, carry more payload, and burn less fuel, the designer must always keep in mind the ease of maintenance, reliability, and support required after the plane is placed in operation. As we say around here, "It's easy to sell a superior aircraft the first time. Provide poor support and there may not be a next time."

DISCOVERY FILE

Testing Airflow

When Orville and Wilbur Wright hit a discouraging slump in their glider experiments sometime in 1901, they began to think that perhaps they were basing their designs on wrong information. They realized they would have to redo the tables on *lift* that had been compiled by others.

They decided to calculate their own tables based on tests of different kinds of wing surfaces. So they built a *wind tunnel.* It would not be the first wind tunnel ever built—the first crude tunnel was built by marine engineer Francis Wenham in 1871—but the Wright's tunnel would be the first to play a role in changing history and launching the Aviation Age. The Wright brother's wind tunnel was primitive. It consisted of an oblong wooden box mounted on a wood frame. It had a fan at one end, and a glass viewing window on top. The brothers made 200 miniature wings to test. Some were curved, others were flat. Some were long and thick, others were short and thin. In the moving stream of air inside their wind tunnel they tested every possible design.

They observed how the wings behaved and compiled new tables. When they were finished, they returned to Kitty Hawk, sure that they had the information needed to succeed.

While the Wright brothers' wind tunnel looked primitive by present standards, the principle is the same today. Wind tunnels are still used to test the effects of wind on aircraft, cars, even houses. While computers today do much of the data analysis (some even simulate wind tunnels), and wind tunnels are extremely sophisticated, testing is still a critical part of the design process. The motto in aviation design is "test first, fly later."

In simple terms, a wind tunnel is a tubelike chamber in which wind is made to flow over the object being tested. A stationary scale model of the device (or the device itself) is placed in the test section of the wind tunnel and connected to instruments. The instruments measure and record the effects of a moving airstream.

Today, no aircraft or spacecraft is built without first being tested in wind tunnels. Data collected tells engineers how aircraft behave under different conditions.

NASA's many wind tunnels can test a full-sized airplane or an object as small as a match. The world's largest wind tunnel is located at NASA's Ames facility in Moffett Field, California. It is large enough to test a Boeing 747. NASA's Icing Research Tunnel at the Lewis Research Center in Cleveland, Ohio, can duplicate in-flight icing conditions so engineers can study how ice forms on aircraft.

The National Transonic Facility at NASA's Langley Research Center in Virginia is a new kind of wind tunnel that uses very cold nitrogen gas to test small models of aircraft as they "fly" through the sound barrier.

PHOTO COURTESY OF NASA

You can build a simple wind tunnel using a box and a fan. Cut out large windows on three sides of the box. Tape clear plastic over the side windows. Place the fan in front of one of the open end windows and leave the other end clear for the wind to exit.

Using a model airplane smaller than the box (or various wing models), design an experiment to compare the effects of a moving airstream. You can either suspend the model from the top of the box—as in the Puppet Plane Science Activity—or use wire and modeling clay to support it at the base. Short lengths of colored string can be taped or tied to the model (the strings will enable you to see the effect of the wind produced by the fan). Observe the patterns made by the strings when the fan runs at various speeds.

Many wind tunnels use smoke to help scientists and engineers see the airstreams. Experiments using smoke should only be tried with supervision of an adult.

Discovery File

Do Jet Contrails Forecast a Cloudy Climate?

Can wispy plumes of jet exhaust affect climate?

That's a question that climatologists are asking as more than 62 million commercial and military flights leave their trails of jet exhaust across the skies above the United States each year.

The short answer is that jet exhaust plumes—commonly referred to as *contrails*—can influence regional climate.

Contrails are a type of cloud formed by two parcels of air. There's warm, wet air from jet exhaust and the frigid air of the upper atmosphere. The resulting process is like seeing your breath on a cold day.

Atmospheric scientist Steven Ackerman of the University of Wisconsin at Madison, has estimated that in certain heavy air-traffic corridors, cloud cover has increased by as much as 20 percent.

Contrails may be small clouds to begin with, but they spread and they can last a long time.

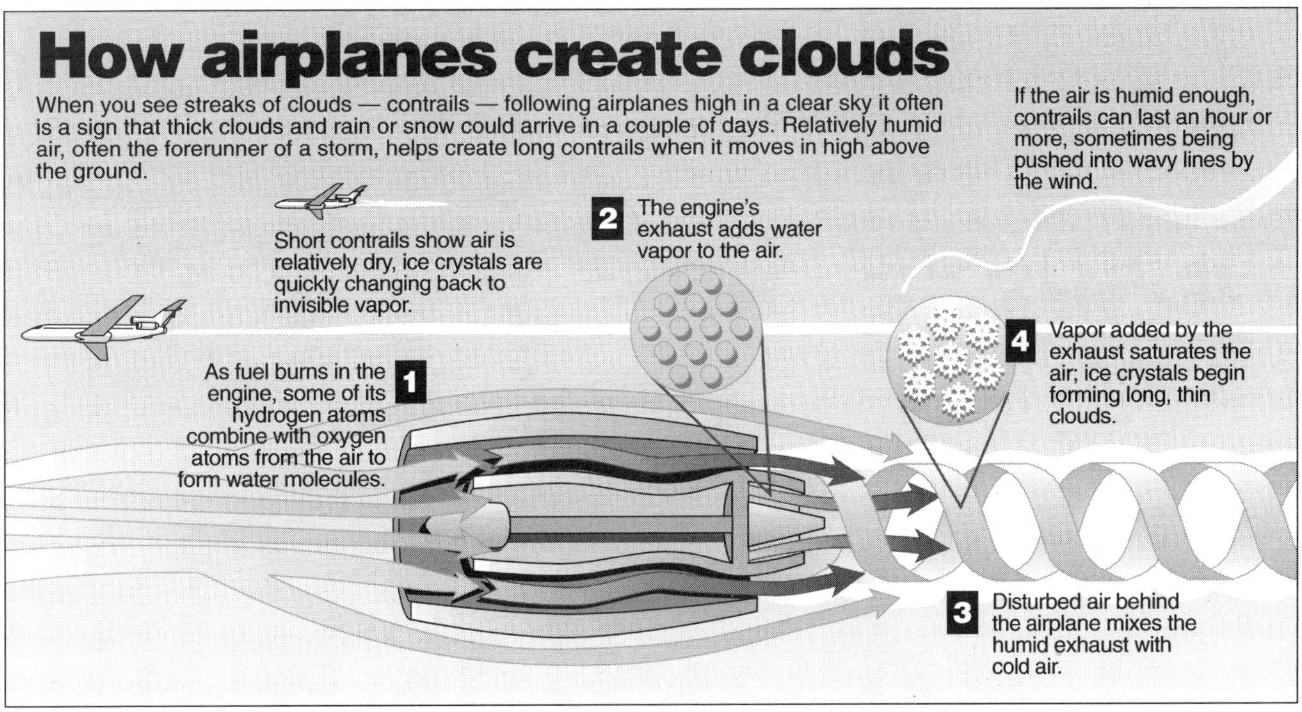

IN THE NEWS

View from the cockpit: A deadly dive

By Paul Hoversten
USA TODAY

PITTSBURGH — From the cockpit of USAir Flight 427, the hills around Pittsburgh rolled smoothly on the horizon as the Boeing 737 cruised at 6,000 feet on approach to the airport.

Gradually, the plane banked to the left, as ground controllers ordered. Then it veered sharply and nose-dived earthward at 300 mph.

It wasn't the real thing, but investigators believe that scenario — a Boeing computer simulation played Monday on a huge screen at the start of the National Transportation Safety Board's hearing — is what the pilots probably saw the evening of Sept. 8 in the nation's deadliest air crash in seven years.

The animated video, based on readings from the plane's flight data recorder, drew gasps from family members and spectators.

"It just took my breath away," says Rose Rubino, a Poland, Ohio, housewife who lost a daughter and son- in-law in the crash.

The investigation into the mystery crash is focusing on the aircraft's tail rudder and possible wind turbulence from a 727 that was flying 4 miles ahead of Flight 427.

Monday's hearing comes after an investigation that has taken an estimated 100,000 man-hours by the safety board, airline, manufacturer, pilots union and other safety experts, said NTSB chairman Jim Hall.

Boeing developed both the cockpit view video and an external view video by reconstructing the 11 flight parameters on the data recorder.

George Green, an engineer at NASA's Langley Research Center at Hampton Roads, Va., told the board that the Boeing 737 probably encountered a "wind vortex," the air turbulence created by another plane's wings.

Green said a vortex could cause a plane to roll or swivel from side to side, but "I don't think there's anything with a vortex strong enough to flip a 737 upside down."

The aircraft's autopilot equipment, along with the rudder controls, normally would help dampen the effects of a vortex. To get out of a severe left roll, a pilot would need to swing the rudder to the right and pull on the cockpit wheel.

But if the rudder was inoperable or stuck to the left, it would cause the plane to continue in a left turn and eventually cause it to go vertical — as happened with Flight 427.

William Perry, head of the FBI's Pittsburgh office, said agents found no evidence of explosives aboard the aircraft and ruled out foul play.

USA TODAY, 24 JANUARY, 1995

IN THE NEWS

Fatalities at the rear of Flight 1288

The two passengers killed Saturday in the Delta Airlines accident in Pensacola, Fla., were seated near the rear of the plane. They were hit by debris when an engine disintegrated as Delta Flight 1288 accelerated for takeoff. Safety experts differ on the safest place to sit. In this incident:

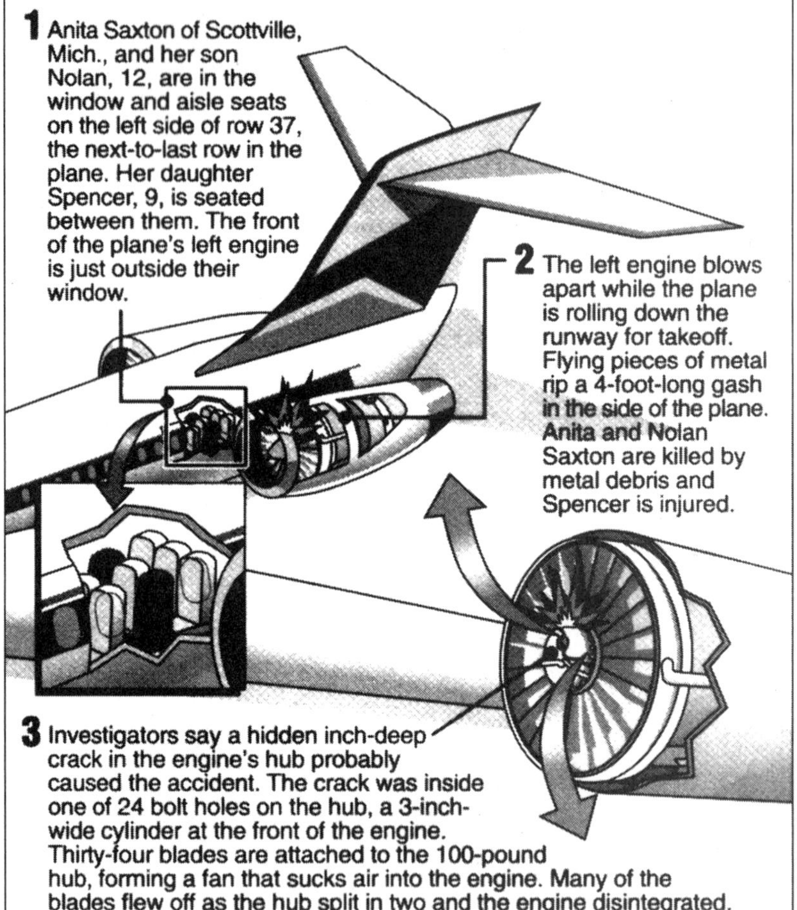

USA TODAY, 10 JULY, 1996

THE STORY—PART 3

Early Fliers and Would-Be Aviators

PHOTO COURTESY OF THE SMITHSONIAN INSTITUTE

Before Kitty Hawk, there were balloons, gliders, and many designs for fantastic contraptions that never flew. There were also kites. Long before the New World was colonized, the Chinese flew kites. In Australia, the Aborigines "flew" boomerangs—flying devices with cambered (curved) surfaces.

Early inventors had little understanding of the principles of flight. They also lacked the power and technology necessary to lift off from the ground. Leonardo da Vinci may have understood some concepts of flight, but he lacked a true understanding of aerodynamics, as well as modern materials, and engine power.

In 1783, Joseph and Étienne Montgolfier loaded a duck, a sheep, and a rooster into a basket. The basket, dangling beneath a hot-air balloon, lifted the animals high into the air. Once the Montgolfier brothers were sure that the animals could breathe the high-altitude air, they launched a man—the first "human aeronaut." The balloon worked, but the brothers didn't really understand why. Do you?

Balloons and gliders are flying machines without engines. For lift, gliders depend on wind, and balloons on their density being lower than that of air. When it came to steering, balloons were at the mercy of the wind, while early gliders were steered by the pilot dangling his legs or shifting his body to redistribute weight.

In the early 1800s, English scientist Sir George Cayley developed and flew the first glider. Cayley, remembered as the "father of aviation," was the first to recognize that fixed, curved wings are better than flapping wings for heavier-than-air craft.

In 1849, a brave ten-year-old boy briefly lifted off the ground in one of Cayley's gliders. Cayley worked out and applied some early principles of lift, drag, and thrust. He also invented the horizontal rudder (elevator).

Later in the 1800s, Otto Lilienthal of Germany, Octave Chanute (a French-born naturalized citizen of the United States), and Samuel Langley of the United States each experimented with gliders. In 1896, the same year Lilienthal died in a glider accident, Langley designed and flew a small, unpiloted, steam-powered aircraft. After Langley's 1903 calamity, people became discouraged and assumed that humans would never fly. Nine days later, the Wright brothers proved them wrong.

The Wright brothers launched the Age of Aviation, and people took to the air. Lighter-than-air craft—like the popular airships of the 1920s—were still being developed at the time of the Wright brothers, but dirigibles and balloons achieved only limited commercial success. And after the fatal 1937 explosion of the Hindenburg, passenger flights in hydrogen-filled dirigibles were stopped.

In World War I, biplanes—with both upper and lower wings—were used on bombing raids and reconnaissance missions. After the war, single wing planes began to replace biplanes, and air mail became the choice for speeding correspondence across the United States. Air shows became popular entertainment as "barnstormers" and "wing walkers" performed daring stunts.

In the 1930s, the commercial airline industry began to grow. Boeing introduced its first modern passenger plane in 1933; the model was so successful it was used for the DC-3.

World War II saw the airplane become the major weapon. It also saw many advancements in aviation. By the end of the war, jet engines had been developed, missiles were in use, and the space race was on.

SCIENCE ACTIVITY

Up Where the Air Is Rare

Purpose

To apply an understanding of the vertical structure of the atmosphere to aircraft safety design.

Background

Many of the clients you will meet at the air show want to know how your airplane will perform at different altitudes. But no one in your company has enough experience in atmospheric science to explain how differences in the air at different altitudes affects the flight of an airplane. No one knows how these altitude differences might affect the design either. You have been selected to represent your company at a special workshop on the subject. It's your responsibility to bring back as much information as possible to help your company answer client's questions.

Materials

- graph paper
- construction paper
- colored pens or pencils

Procedure

How do the *thickness* and *temperature* of air change as you go higher in altitude? Have you ever driven to the top of a mountain? Have you flown on an airplane? Or, have you been in an elevator to the top of a very tall building? In your expert group, discuss the experiences you have had and what changes you sensed as you climbed higher and higher. Appoint a recorder to list the experiences of the group, then write an explanation of each experience, if you know it. You will return to this list later in the activity.

The following data table shows what happens to the pressure and the temperature of air as altitude increases. The figures are average for the world, so they may not be exactly the same everywhere. You will need to take back to your company a set of graphs that show this data.

Altitude (km)	Pressure of Air (as % of surface pressure)	Average Temp (C°)
0	100%	15°
2	79%	3°
4	61%	-9°
6	48%	-22°
8	36%	-35°
10	26%	-48°
12	19%	-56°
14	15%	-56°
16	10%	-56°
18	8%	-56°
20	6%	-56°
22	5%	-54°
24	4%	-52°
26	3%	-50°
28	2%	-48°
30	1.5%	-46°
32	1%	-44°

The middle column shows the percent of normal air pressure for the altitudes listed in the left column. For example, at 0 km, air pressure is at its maximum. As you rise to 2 km, air pushes on surfaces at only 79% of its sea level maximum. At 2 km there is 21% less force. Look below for a different example of the same idea.

After you finish your graph presentations, answer the conclusion questions.

Conclusion

1. Think about a small child holding a helium balloon. It slips out of her hand and drifts upward into the air. What will eventually happen to the balloon? Explain your answer.
2. In many old airplanes the area where the pilot sat—the cockpit— was open. (In modern airplanes, this area is enclosed.) The pilot often didn't even have a windshield to protect him from the environment. Why would an open cockpit limit the altitude at which the airplane could fly?
3. Passenger jet airliners cruise at an altitude of 10–12 kilometers. But above 4 kilometers humans begin to feel ill, and above 6 kilometers most humans lose the ability to think clearly and even lose consciousness. Why do you think this happens? How are jetliners designed to provide safe air travel to passengers even when they fly above 10 kilometers?
4. Review the list of experiences and explanations you and your group made at the beginning of this activity. If you can add to the list, or if you need to change your explanations in light of what you now know about the atmosphere, make your changes in another color, or use a different font in your word processing application. Which of your experiences would you use with your clients to show them you understand the structure of the atmosphere?

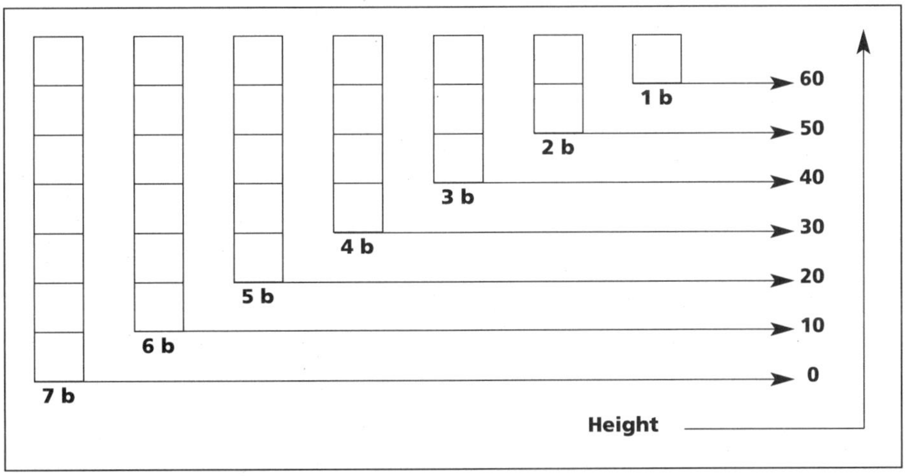

The diagram shows what a column of air might look like if you could see it in little boxes. The arrows show the height (no units). The left has 7 boxes. Let's say it weighs 7 b (boxes) at a height of 0. The second one has a weight of 6 b at a height of 10. The third column weighs 5 b at 20, and so on. Notice that as you get higher, the columns of air weigh less! That's because you are rising above the boxes below.

Famous Fliers

Eddie Rickenbacker (1890–1973)

American World War I flying ace Eddie Rickenbacker started out as an automobile racer, then volunteered for the Army flying service in 1917. He shot down 22 enemy planes and four balloons in World War I. The most decorated American combat pilot of the war, he later served as president of Eastern Airlines (1938–1959). During the time Rickenbacker was president, Eastern Airlines grew into one of the nation's major passenger carriers. Eastern Airlines went bankrupt in 1994.

PHOTO COURTESY OF THE SMITHSONIAN INSTITUTE

Baron Manfred von Richthofen (1892–1918)

A World War I German fighter pilot, Richthofen gained fame as the "Red Baron" because he flew a red Fokker triplane. The flying ace died after two years of combat flying. Before he died, the Red Baron shot down 80 Allied planes in air-to-air combat called "dogfights."

Glenn Hammond Curtiss (1878–1930)

An inventor and aviator, Curtiss started out as a bicycle mechanic and motorcycle racer. Then he began to build engines for the first U.S. dirigibles. He began to experiment with and ultimately made important contributions to the development of aircraft.

In 1908, *Scientific American* magazine sponsored a contest to find a pilot who could fly a kilometer. Curtiss won the trophy.

Curtiss built and flew the first successful seaplane in 1911—after showing the U.S. Navy that planes could take off and land from ships—and built the first flying boat the next year. Curtiss is also given credit for inventing the *aileron*, the hinged flaps on the trailing edge of an airplane's wings. Curtiss's aileron concept was the subject of a patent fight with the Wright brothers. They claimed that the aileron was an infringement on wing warping—their patented method of twisting the wings to control *roll.*

"Lucky Lindy" — Charles A. Lindbergh (1902–1974)

Charles A. Lindbergh, son of a Congressman, grew up to become America's most famous aviator of the early 20th century. Born in Detroit, Lindbergh began dreaming of flying at a very young age—just as the Aviation Age began—and finally learned to fly when he was 20. He started college to become an engineer,

PHOTO COURTESY OF THE SMITHSONIAN INSTITUTE

but left after two years to become a barnstormer—a pilot who performed daring aviation stunts at fairs.

By 1925, Lindbergh was flying a mail route between Chicago and St. Louis, when he learned of the $25,000 prize being offered for the person who made the first solo flight across the Atlantic Ocean. He persuaded a group of St. Louis businessmen to pay for a plane so he could enter the contest. He called the specially designed plane the *Spirit of St. Louis.*

At 7:52 A.M. on May 20, 1927, Lindbergh left Roosevelt Field, Long Island, loaded with 450 gallons of fuel. He reached Le Bourget airport near Paris, at 10:21 P.M. (French time) on May 21. Lindbergh had flown over 3,600 miles in 33½ hours. Called the "lone eagle," he returned home a hero. Other pilots had crossed the Atlantic before Lindbergh, but none had accomplished this feat alone and nonstop.

Despite ice on the wings, fatigue, and limited vision—he used a periscope to see forward, Lindbergh landed with 84 gallons of fuel left. Lindbergh flew so low over fishermen in the Atlantic near Britain that he called out to them, "Which way is Ireland?" as he swooped over the startled men.

Lindbergh was thrust into the spotlight again a few years later. In what was called the "crime of the century," the baby son of Charles and Anne Morrow Lindbergh was kidnapped from their New Jersey home. A ransom was paid for the baby's safe return, but he was later found murdered. This tragic episode has been dramatized in movies and television.

Lindbergh spent his later years as a consultant to aircraft and airline industries.

PHOTO COURTESY OF THE SMITHSONIAN INSTITUTE

Amelia Earhart (1897–1937)

The first woman to fly solo over the Atlantic Ocean has been the subject of many dramas and much speculation.

Born in Kansas, Earhart served as a nurse's aide in Canada during World War I. While in Canada she became interested in flying. During her life Amelia Earhart accomplished many firsts in aviation history as either pilot or copilot. She was the first woman to fly over the Atlantic as a passenger and, in 1932, the first woman to cross the Atlantic solo—five years after Lindbergh's solo flight.

By the fall of 1934, ten pilots had already lost their lives attempting to fly across the Pacific from Hawaii to California. Amelia's successful attempt was a first in aviation history. It was also the first time a civilian pilot used a two-way radio telephone to communicate with the ground. But Amelia's lasting fame came from her final flight.

In July 1937, Earhart set off with navigator Fred Noonan to fly around the world. The tour was well-publicized. People around the world followed her progress. Sadly and inexplicably, her plane disappeared after taking off from New Guinea. A search failed to find any trace of the plane or its occupants.

A team from a historical aircraft association returned to the island where Earhart and Noonan were thought to have landed. The searchers discovered a few items, which they identified as possibly belonging to Earhart. Speculation continues to this day, over whether Earhart simply ran out of fuel, was captured by the Japanese, or died on a Pacific island.

Charles E. "Chuck" Yeager (1923–   )

Chuck Yeager was the first American to fly an aircraft faster than the speed of sound. Born in West Virginia, Yeager enlisted in the Army in 1941, and was assigned to the Army Air Corps—forerunner to the U.S. Air Force. As a fighter pilot in World War II , he flew 64 missions and shot down 13 enemy aircraft. He became an Air Force test pilot after the war.

Pilots and others in the aviation industry long believed that breaking the sound barrier was impossible. When pilots approached the speed of sound, their planes encountered violent turbulence and often disintegrated from the extreme pounding.

Yeager took on the hazardous assignment of making the first flight in the experimental Bell X-1. On October 14, 1947—launched from the belly of a B-29 bomber over the Mojave Desert in Nevada—the orange X-1 broke the sound barrier by traveling at Mach 1.07. In 1953, Yeager set another record when he flew at 2½ times the speed of sound in the Bell X-1A.

IN THE NEWS

747 called safe, trustworthy jet

By Keith L. Alexander
USA TODAY

Boeing's 747 changed aviation when it was introduced in 1970, launching an era of moderately priced travel for middle-class consumers on both sides of the Atlantic.

A quarter-century later, the double-deck, hump-backed 747 is one of aviation's most popular wide-body jets. Boeing has delivered 1,082 747s and has orders for 124 of its latest model, the 747-400.

The TWA 747-100 that crashed Wednesday was delivered in 1971 and had 360 seats. Later generations of the 747 were bigger. The current model, the 747-400, can carry up to 450 people and sells for $150 million to $180 million each.

It's also one of the industry's most trustworthy planes, says stock analyst Bill Whitlow of Pacific Crest Securities. "My gut feeling says it's a pretty safe airplane," he says.

The 747, including the original 747-100, has had an average of 1.64 major accidents per million departures, compared with an industry average of 1.83 per million departures.

Corrosion may be trouble spot

Service reports filed with the government for the Boeing 747 that crashed show it had at least 40 reports of corrosion, part failures and other problems between 1988 and 1994. Former 747 pilot Charles Smith, who reviewed the reports, said they were consistent with a plane 25 years old, but 10 cases of corrosion might be cause for concern.

The jumbo jet and its history

The jet that was TWA Flight 800 had two operators in its 25-year history: TWA and Iran.

The Boeing 747-100

- **Aircraft type:** Four-engine, two-level jet with bulge behind cockpit
- **Seating:** Capacity varies, but a typical three-class seating configuration can hold 366 passengers
- **On board:** 212 passengers and 18 crew members
- **Part replaced:** An engine pressure ratio gauge was replaced in the cockpit before the plane took off from New York. The instrument provides the cockpit crew throttle data during takeoffs.
- **Its history:** The jet that crashed Wednesday night was ordered by Eastern Airlines in 1967, but never was delivered. It was ordered by TWA on May 1, 1970, and delivered on Oct. 27, 1971. On Dec. 15, 1975, TWA sold the plane to Boeing, which sold it to the Imperial Iranian Air Force on the same day. One year and a day later, on Dec. 16, 1976, the plane was sold back to TWA.

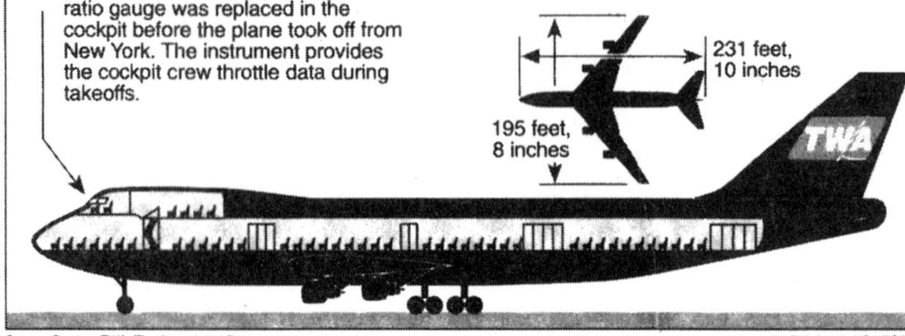

Source: Boeing, TWA, The Associated Press

By Bob Laird, USA TODAY

Some 747s have been involved in well-known incidents. The Pan Am jet that was bombed over Scotland by terrorists in 1988 was a 747. A bomb was the suspected cause of an Air India 747's crash off the Irish coast in 1985.

Seventeen 747s have been destroyed in crashes, not counting those destroyed by sabotage or military action.

The 747 was involved in two big aviation disasters: a 1977 runway collision of two jets that killed 583 people and a 1985 crash that killed 524. Both were blamed on human error.

Two accidents led Boeing to redesign the plane's engine mounts, which hold the 747's four engines to the wings: On Oct. 4, 1992, an El Al 747 crashed into an apartment building in Amsterdam, and on Dec. 21, 1991, a China Airlines 747 crashed in Taiwan. In each case, an engine ripped away from the wing after takeoff.

Since 1993, the Federal Aviation Administration has required airlines to make regular ultrasonic and visual inspections of the engine mounts.

C.O. Miller, a former aviation accident investigator, says it's possible the engine mounts were involved in Wednesday's crash. "It's certainly possible. Anyone who says these things can't happen hasn't been around the block."

Boeing spokeswoman Liz Verdier says Boeing is working with investigators to determine the cause of the crash. Verdier says Boeing is also looking into the dates of TWA's last examination of its engine mounts.

But Clive Irving, author of *Wide Body: The Story of the 747*, says he doesn't suspect the mounts because the explosion was "too instantaneous."

USA TODAY, 19 JULY, 1996

STUDENT VOICES

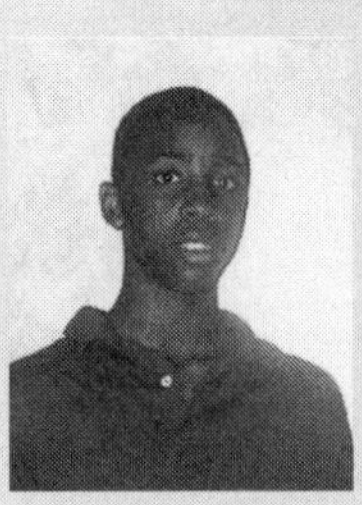

Mr. Taffel thought it would be fun for me to learn to fly. He talked to me about wind speed, how much weight you can have in an airplane, the amount of fuel it needs, and how to fix a few of its parts. I know I want to fly again, but I don't think flying will be a part of my career.

DAMON EASLEY
BALTIMORE, MD

Discovery File

The Tuskegee Airmen

People learning about World War II sometimes miss a very special feat of patriotism and bravery. The combat achievements of the African American pilots of the 332nd Fighter Group, *The Tuskegee Airmen*, were special. Their story is a shining example of courageous men, overcoming the prejudice and discrimination of the 1940s, to serve their country in time of war.

About 1,000 Americans of African ancestry completed their flight training at Tuskegee Army Air Field, Tuskegee, Alabama. Despite many obstacles, 445 went oversees as combat pilots. They served in the European Theater of Operations including North Africa, and the Mediterranean. Flying "bomber escort" and ground attack on 15,533 sorties between May, 1943, and June 9, 1945, the Tuskegee Airmen compiled an enviable combat record. None of the bombers they escorted was lost to enemy fighters, they destroyed 251 enemy aircraft, and they won more than 850 medals. But their record was not without losses. Sixty-six of the Tuskegee Airmen were killed in action.

PHOTO COURTESY OF CULVER PICTURES INC

Some Tuskegee Airmen pilots

PHOTO COURTESY OF US AIR FORCE DAVA STILL MEDIA DEPT.

Benjamin O. Davis, Jr.

On March 24, 1945, Colonel Benjamin Davis, Jr. (he became a four-star general in 1998), took the lead as seventy-two fighters from the 332nd left their base at Ramitelli, Italy. Their mission was to escort bombers on one leg of their flight to an important target: Berlin, Germany. When the relief squadron failed to appear, Colonel Davis and the rest of the 332nd were getting low on fuel, but they pressed on. As the bombers approached Berlin, German fighters appeared. The pilots of the 332nd shot down three of the attacking German Me-262s, but lost two of their P-51s. One of the downed American planes was piloted by Captain Armour McDaniels. He was taken prisoner and held until a few months later when the Allies freed prisoners of war.

For their gallant efforts, the 332nd was awarded the Distinguished Unit Citation.

The legacy of the Tuskegee Airmen was the eventual desegregation of the United States Air Force, a recognition that black pilots are equal to white pilots, and the respect and admiration earned by former Tuskegee pilots like General Benjamin Davis, Jr. and General Daniel "Chappie" James.

IN THE NEWS

229 killed in 747 crash

TWA flight to Paris goes down like 'fireball' off N.Y.

By Steve Marshall
and David Field
USA TODAY

A TWA 747-100 jetliner carrying 229 people exploded in midair and crashed into the Atlantic Ocean shortly after takeoff from New York's JFK Airport on Wednesday night.

The Coast Guard said no one survived the crash.

Flight 800, en route to Paris, had just taken off when it plunged into the water off Moriches Inlet.

President Clinton expressed "deep concern" and was monitoring developments, a White House spokesman said.

"I thought it was a stunt plane and then it burst into flames, and burst into flames again and hit the water. A couple minutes later, we heard what sounded like thunder and felt a strong vibration," surfer Chris Clapp said.

"It was a big orange fireball. . . . You saw nothing but flames," said witness Eileen Daly. "My initial reaction was what is it. Oh my God, it's an airplane!"

"Bodies are starting to turn up," said Coast Guard spokesman John Chindblom.

Neither the FBI nor the FAA would comment about the possibility of a bomb, though terrorism expert Larry Johnson told CNN a bomb could have been the cause.

But Jim Hall, chairman of the NTSB, told CNN, "Until we have the facts, I won't speculate as to what caused the accident. We will find out the cause and report it to the American people.

"At this point, we do not have any additional information. We have launched a team of people. They will be there in hours."

An FAA airport security advisory committee met Wednesday afternoon, and participants told USA TODAY that the panel had decided to heighten security at certain airports.

The FAA confirmed that the committee had met but would not discuss details of its actions or agenda.

FAA spokesman Eliot Brener said the agency's Boston air traffic control center lost radar contact with the TWA plane at 8:45 p.m., when it was 20 miles southeast of Long Island.

Some reports put the plane at 8,000 feet at the time.

USA TODAY, 218 JULY, 1996

IN THE NEWS

Aircraft rudder operation

A rudder malfunction is one of the possibilities being investigated in two Boeing 737 airliner crashes. The rudder's role in an airplane turn:

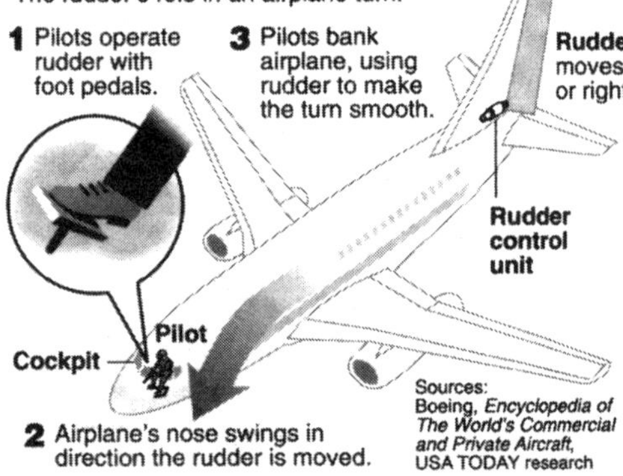

Sources: Boeing, *Encyclopedia of The World's Commercial and Private Aircraft*, USA TODAY research

By Sam Ward, USA TODAY

Faulty rudder repairs found on 36 jetliners

By Dennis Cauchon
USA TODAY

The Boeing 737 rudder — the focus of two crash probes — was ill-repaired on 36 planes, federal regulators say.

The problem rudders were replaced Wednesday on two foreign aircraft. The changes on those in the United States were finished last weekend.

Bad repairs could have caused a plane to move in the opposite direction from what the pilot wanted, the Federal Aviation Administration said.

The pilots of two airplanes reported that the rudders had responded "sluggishly," said FAA spokeswoman Diane Spitaliere. The rudder's hydraulic power control units were removed and failed tests.

The 36 faulty rudders were on America West, Southwest Airlines, Alaska Air and federal government planes.

In all, about 3,000 Boeing 737s are flying.

The Boeing 737 rudder is a suspect in two earlier crashes. But the FAA said the latest problem isn't related to earlier questions about the rudder.

The two unsolved crashes:

▶ A USAir Boeing 737-300 went down in Pittsburgh in September, killing 132. "We had an unexplained movement of the rudder. We still don't know why," said Michael Benson of the National Transportation Safety Board.

▶ A United Airlines 737-200 crash in Colorado Springs in March 1991 killed 25. The NTSB cited the rudder and weather as possible factors, but no specific cause was found.

The FAA ordered airlines to replace the power control units on all Boeing 737 rudders, starting in January 1994.

Aero Controls Inc., an FAA-certified repair shop in Auburn, Wash., had recently made the changes on the 36.

The FAA said the wrong tool was used. Aero said tests found the tools were proper.

The mistake "was in our shop, but the specific cause isn't understood," said Brian Thomas, quality assurance director at Aero Controls.

USA TODAY, 16 MARCH, 1995

DISCOVERY FILE

Why Planes Crash

Statistically, flying is safer than other forms of transportation, especially driving automobiles.

Unfortunately, when airplanes are involved in accidents, sometimes there is major loss of life. Plane crash events are dramatic and tragic. They are the subject of headlines and stories on prime-time television.

Metal fatigue, flocks of geese, bombs, microbursts, human error—all have played roles in airplane accidents. Plane crashes are caused by four main factors: weather, human error, mechanical failure, and sabotage—or some combination of these.

As safe as flying is, weather is unpredictable and creates forces that cause aircraft to behave in unexpected ways. Weather can change quickly and without warning. Increasingly sophisticated equipment like *Doppler radar* is being installed in airports to help pilots know when wind conditions make it unsafe to fly.

Weather-related problems include: *wing icing* on the ground and in flight, *wind shear*, thunderstorms, and other severe weather. Forces created by severe weather are unseen and often unpredictable. Some of these forces, like wind shear, are only beginning to be understood.

Wind shear, especially in its most deadly form called a *microburst*, can drop a plane hundreds of feet in seconds. Lift and drag are both somewhat dependent on wing shape; even a thin layer of ice can change the shape of the wing, creating turbulence instead of lift. New technology and recent research is giving us many more tools so that aviation can become even safer than it is.

Icy buildup on its wings caused the Washington, DC, crash of AirFlorida Flight 90 in January 1982. That crash may have been caused by bad weather, but human error was also to blame. Pilots make the decision to fly or stay at the gate. They can also request additional de-icing. However, a millimeter thickness of ice is hard to see from the cockpit window. The AirFlorida pilots made the decision to take off, when they should have requested deicing. That decision cost lives.

Human error also played the key role in the tragic crash of ValuJet 592 on May 1, 1996. After considerable searching in the Everglades, investigators discovered evidence that mislabeled canisters of oxygen were being carried in the cargo area. The canisters had been marked "empty" when they were not. Empty oxygen canisters are considered safe. When the same canisters are not empty, they are considered *hazardous material*, and hazardous material is not allowed in the cargo hold of a passenger airplane. The chemicals in these mislabeled oxygen canisters created an exothermic—heat-producing—chemical reaction that led to a fire and explosion in ValuJet 592.

The entire world followed the investigation into the mid-air explosion of TWA Flight 800. On the evening of July 17, 1996, the 373,000-pound Boeing 747 broke into pieces and fell from the night sky into the waters off eastern Long Island. The investigation focused on three possible causes: mechanical failure, a missile, or a bomb.

Despite an intensive search for clues, as of October 1997, there was no conclusive evidence as to the cause of the crash of TWA Flight 800. Sometimes it takes years for FAA investigators to reach a conclusion. And sometimes, as in the crash near Pittsburgh of USAir Flight 427 in 1994, the cause cannot be determined. (Clues from the USAir Flight 427 crash point to a rudder problem found in other Boeing 737s.)

A crash in October 1996 of Aeroperu Flight 603 en route to Chile was apparently caused by the failure of its navigational system.

Sabotage as an act of terrorism caused the Pan Am Flight 103 explosion over Lockerbie, Scotland, in 1988. Piecing together the smallest fragments, investigators traced the cause to a bomb that had been smuggled aboard the plane in a small radio-cassette player.

Fortunately for the millions of passengers who fly for business or pleasure, airplane accidents are very rare; and, as unfortunate as airplane disasters are for the victims and their families, they often provide lessons that help prevent future accidents from happening.

DISCOVERY FILE

Two Booms for the Price of One

Two sonic booms accompany the space shuttle when it returns to Earth. The shuttle produces shock waves as it passes through the atmosphere, just like any other aircraft traveling faster than the speed of sound.

A sonic boom is created by rapid change in air pressure. As an airplane travels through air, it pushes air molecules aside, compressing and deflecting them. With subsonic flight, the sound of an approaching craft make the air molecules begin to move aside even before the plane arrives. However, when a plane travels faster than sound, the air molecules have no warning. The collision between the air and the supersonic plane produces shock waves. A sonic boom is what is heard when the pressure built up by the shock wave is released.

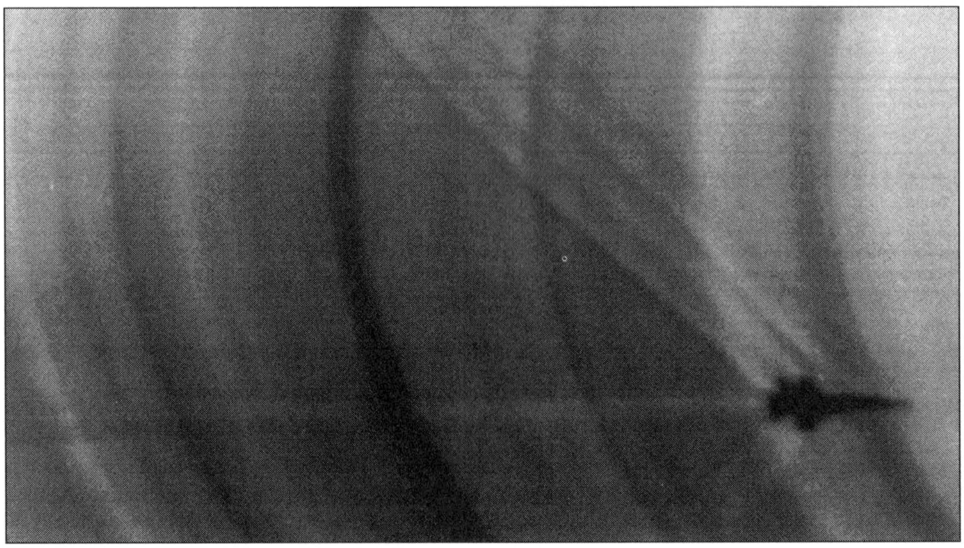

PHOTO COURTESY OF NASA

With a returning space shuttle the shock waves form cones—one at each end. This causes two sonic booms—one from the nose, one from the tail. Smaller fighter aircraft also produce twin booms, but the human ear hears only one. The shuttle is longer, so the time between the booms is longer and thus more distinct.

Weight, size, and shape of an aircraft, its altitude and flight path, as well as weather or atmospheric conditions, all affect sonic booms.

STUDENT VOICES

I was scared the first time I flew. We got up to 1300 feet really fast. Mr. Taffel took his hands off the controls and told me to steer. When we landed, and didn't crash, it made me feel freer. Flying has taught me to do better in my classes, and always be prepared.

JASON KEMPA
BALTIMORE, MD

Discovery File

Flying Faster Than Sound

Until 1947, no one believed that an airplane could fly faster than the speed of sound and survive. During World War II, fighter pilots talked about the hazards of "breaking the sound barrier" or flying faster than the speed of sound. Breaking the sound barrier became a real challenge.

Airplanes approaching the speed of sound in the 1940s lost control and sometimes disintegrated. The transition from *subsonic* (less than the speed of sound) to *supersonic* (faster than the speed of sound) caused structural vibrations that literally tore the wings off.

As aircraft reach the critical transition from subsonic to supersonic speeds, conditions change. A new set of aerodynamic problems arise. At this point (in what is called the *transonic* region), air is rushing past different parts of the aircraft at varying speeds, affecting lift and drag. Shock waves begin to form. Drag increases significantly. Turbulence can throw an airplane out of control.

High flying speeds are measured in what is called *Mach* numbers—named for Austrian physicist Ernst Mach. Traveling at the speed of sound would be *Mach 1*; twice the speed of sound, *Mach 2;* and so on.

Speeds less than Mach 0.8 are called subsonic (air flows slower than sound over all parts of the plane). About Mach 0.8 to Mach 1.2 is referred to as *transonic.* Above Mach 1.2, or supersonic, air flows faster than sound over the entire plane. At these speeds, sudden increases in air pressure create shock waves out in front of the plane. The faster the speed, the more intense are these pressure waves. (Shock waves are heard on the ground as loud sonic booms.) Heat becomes a critical factor at speeds greater than Mach 5, in what is called the hypersonic range.

PHOTO COURTESY OF THE SMITHSONIAN INSTITUTE

The *speed of sound* varies with temperature. At sea level, it is 760 mph or 1,226 km/h; above seven miles altitude, it drops to 660 mph or 1,062 km/h.

Manufacturers designed experimental aircraft to combat the aerodynamic challenges of higher speeds, and in 1947, test pilot Charles E. "Chuck" Yeager flew such a mission in a new research aircraft.

The experimental Bell X-1, a bright orange rocket plane that could fly for just two-and-a-half minutes, had to be launched from another plane. Yeager took the Bell X-1 to a speed of 1,127 kilometers (700 miles) per hour, Mach 1.06, at an altitude of 13,000 meters (43,000 feet), and to even greater speeds in later flights. The sound barrier had been broken.

Though today, military aircraft with their swept-back wings routinely fly at speeds faster than the speed of sound, the most well-known commercial aircraft to do so is the Concorde, the supersonic jet that cruises at Mach 2 (1,354 mph or 2,180 km/h). The delta-shaped wings of the Concorde stay inside the shock wave and maintain control at supersonic speeds. (Because of the noise they produce, aircraft like the Concorde do not fly at supersonic speeds over populated areas.)

The space shuttle slows down to Mach 5 when it reenters Earth's atmosphere. Proposals are on the drawing board for commercial aircraft that could fly at Mach 5. The experimental reusable launch vehicle, the Lockheed X-33, is being designed to reach Mach 25 (18,000 mph) in orbit.

On the Job

Aircraft Maintenance Technician

Peter S. Pierpont
Embry-Riddle Aeronautical University

When someone flies into town in a $6 million jet, the pilot who climbs down out of that jet is looking for much more than a "wrench turner." Today, much more is expected in terms of communications and other skills from "mechanics." The job has become multidimensional. The men and women who work on planes today are called aircraft maintenance technicians.

A year ago I was a test pilot at a factory in Wyoming; today I'm a professor at Embry-Riddle teaching aerobatics and other courses. As a test pilot, I was more comfortable testing the airplanes because I was a mechanic. When an engine dropped out of a plane I was flying, I knew what to do.

I began working as a technician in the field because I had my own aerobatics school. I like to work with my hands, so I earned what is now called the Airframe and Power Plant Mechanic's certificate. (The FAA is changing the title to Aircraft Maintenance Technician.)

Technology is driving the changes and expanding demands on technicians. You can't go out there with just a wrench anymore. You have to be computer literate. Test equipment is becoming increasingly sophisticated; virtually all the systems involve computer-based testing. As one example, the critical component in a jet engine is fuel, and the fuel control for a jet engine is now called FADEC (Full Authority Digital Engine Control).

Technicians have to know solid-state electronics and digital systems. Of course they have to know cockpit instruments, as well. We're not using instruments anymore; everything is projected on TV screens, which means the technician is working with very sophisticated software. And we are doing more fly-by-wire. You move a stick and it goes to computers along fiber optics, which tell the controls what to do.

Technicians today do many things on the job—installing engines, changing tires, repairing composite structures, working on aircraft electric and hydraulic systems, working on engines and jet engines. An area of growing interest is *composites*, like the materials used to make skis and golf clubs. These materials are used more and more on aircraft. Being able to work with composites is a requirement. Not only must a technician have good mechanical aptitude and understand about torque wrenches, but he or she also must understand about regulations and paperwork.

When I was 17, I enlisted in the Navy. I used to be able to go out and check the engines and start them. I always wanted to be able to just keep on going. I've always loved aviation and went on to try engineering because I liked hands-on stuff. After I finished the undergraduate program, I went on to a graduate program in electrical engineering, which was fun. I went back to school later to get my mechanics qualifications, because I thought as an engineer I was somewhat incomplete, and I wasn't close enough to the hardware—the airplane.

To become a technician, you can go to FAA-approved schools like Embry-Riddle or Purdue. You also can attend junior colleges that offer a technical program. Or, you can work under an approved mechanic as an apprentice. Then you have to take written and oral tests from the FAA and demonstrate your skill in a practical exam. The FAA could walk you over to an airplane and ask you to explain these circuits or take you to a workbench and tell you to install a new injection system on this engine.

We have a 2,270-hour program or five semesters of school

to get a technician's certificate. At our school, students can add two years to the technician's certificate for an undergraduate degree that may help them move into management. A degree in technology makes someone very attractive to corporate aviation. If a corporate jet breaks down in Timbuktu, the company sends over a generator, the technician fixes the engine and flies home. We have a program that produces pilot-mechanics. Those who really love aviation and flying will seek that dimension.

Technicians play an important role on the design team. Designers and engineers need to look at the plane from a technician's point of view. The goal is to design an airplane that is easier to maintain and also costs less. The technician asks questions as the design of airplane moves along because the technician will have to work on it. The team will also ask questions of the technician: How can we design this aircraft for effective maintenance? Is the airplane being built maintainable? Can you get at the engine? Can you get at the electronic controls? Is the airplane designed for maintenance?

You want to consider the maintenance-technician interface or human factor side of things, too. Where are the panels located? Are they friendly? Do you have to climb up a ladder? Can you access panels from inside the plane? Has due regard been giving to high voltages and toxic materials? Is it safe for mechanics to work around? Is the plane serviceable? Can we get the hose up to the fueling ports on the wings?

A maintenance technician has to become more and more familiar with nondestructive testing. In other words, we want to test a component of plane but we don't want to break it!

DISCOVERY FILE

Flight Safety: The Story Statistics Tell

Each day in the United States, more than 30,000 flights are completed safely. This means about 500 million passengers fly on 12 million flights each year. Comparatively speaking, statistics show that flying is significantly safer than other modes of transportation.

Statistics tell us that the leading cause of death in the United States for every age from five through 32 years old is from motor vehicle accidents.

Traffic and Transportation Safety Facts

- 41,798 people were killed in motor vehicle accidents (a 3% increase from 1994) in the United States in 1995—this is equivalent to 114.5 people dying each day.
- 99 out of 100 people injured in the U.S. transportation system are injured in motor vehicle crashes—over three million people.
- Alcohol is the leading factor that contributes to fatal crashes; alcohol-related traffic fatalities increased to 17,274 in 1995 from 16,589 in 1994, an increase of 4%
- In 1966, the traffic fatality rate (deaths per 100 million vehicle miles traveled) was 5.5 deaths. This rate dropped to 1.7 deaths in 1993, thanks to the use of seatbelts, car seats, and motorcycle helmets. The rate has remained constant since.
- Motorcycle fatalities (over 2000) accounted for about 5% of the total—the fatality rate for motorcycles is about 16 times that of passenger cars.
- Overall, traffic fatalities are on the rise.
- Traffic fatalities account for more than 90% of transportation-related deaths.
- In the U.S. railroad industry, highway rail crossings are responsible for half the railroad fatalities that occur each year.
- Fatalities at railroad crossings are on a downward trend, from 615 in 1994 to 579 in 1995 and a projected 418 in 1996.
- By comparison, in 1995, total fatalities from accidents involving scheduled U.S. airline carriers fell to 175 deaths from 264 in 1994.
- General aviation—small private plane—deaths in the U.S. in 1995 totaled 732.
- The U.S. air traffic system, the safest and most complex in the world, handles 82 million air traffic operations annually (roughly two flights per second).
- Worldwide, 557 passengers lost their lives in scheduled flights in 1995.
- The death rate per 100 million passenger miles in 1995 in the world was 0.04, a decrease from the previous year.
- The Flight Safety Foundation predicts that air traffic will double, even triple in volume, over the next two decades.

Sources: National Center for Statistics and Analysis, National Safety Council; *The 1996 World Almanac and Book of Facts*; National Highway Transportation Safety Administration, Bureau of Transportation Statistics, U.S. Department of Transportation

STUDENT VOICES

My first time flying was a wonderful experience, and I'd like to do it again. Mr. Taffel allowed me to take the controls and make a complete circle in the air. It was a great feeling. I don't want to become a pilot though. I want to be a graphic artist, but I might end up designing planes and advertisements for them.

JASON JEFFERYS
BALTIMORE, MD

Soaring

Hang gliding may be the closest people will come to flying like birds.

The modern sport of hang gliding owes a lot to 19th century aerodynamic pioneers Sir George Cayley and Otto Lilienthal. Cayley recognized that the key to flight is not flapping wings, but fixed, curved ones. Lilienthal studied the flight of birds for many years and designed gliders based on his observations. He built and flew hundreds of gliders until 1896, when, at the age of 48, he died of injuries from a gliding accident.

Some of Lilienthal's gliders looked a lot like today's hang gliders, but there are critical differences. For starters, the materials he used were quite different. Lilienthal's gliders were made of wood, cotton, and canvas. Today's hang gliders are made of lightweight materials like aluminum alloys, fiberglass, and synthetics fabrics.

Today's hang gliders do operate on the same principles developed by Cayley and Lilienthal more than a century ago. Photos and illustrations of Lilienthal in flight show him hanging from the wing, his legs dangling into the air. By shifting his body, he steered the glider. Likewise, pilots of the first 20th Century hang gliders also dangled their legs from the wing. Today however, hang glider pilots wrap most of their bodies in flight bags. This reduces drag and enables them to stay aloft longer without getting cold and tired.

PHOTO COURTESY OF THE SMITHSONIAN INSTITUTE

Attached to the wing by a harness, and hanging below the glider's center of gravity, the pilot can make the craft turn, climb, or dive by shifting his or her body weight. At takeoff, the pilot is attached to the frame of the glider. Facing into the wind, the pilot runs forward until the wing fills with air, lifting the apparatus and pilot into the sky. A hang glider can use thermals—rising currents of warm air—to make flights of over 100 miles.

The sport of hang gliding originated in a National Aeronautics and Space Administration (NASA) research project into a vehicle that would return space capsules after reentry into Earth's atmosphere. Dr. Francis Rogallo designed a delta-shaped (triangular) kite for this purpose in the 1950s. People soon began designing hang gliders based on his design. In flight, Rogallo's wing becomes an airfoil with low lift and drag—perfect for gliding.

Although Rogallo's innovation was not utilized for its original purpose, and NASA found other ways to carry spacecraft back to Earth, the engineer inadvertently helped invent a popular aerial sport. All the hang glider enthusiast needs is equipment and a hill or cliff and some good winds—as well as some athletic ability, confidence, and know-how of aerodynamics. A little raw courage doesn't hurt, either!

Top tips for rookie travelers

USA TODAY Road Warriors — business travelers who fly 100,000 miles a year or stay in hotels at least 100 nights a year — share their top travel tips for new frequent travelers:

▶ **Buy easy-to-carry luggage.** Veteran Road Warriors recommend using a carry-on bag with wheels, which makes it easy to zip through airports. Use a garment bag that can be hung up so suits and dresses don't wrinkle. Always pack a change of clothes and essential toiletries in your carry-on in case luggage is lost.

Join frequent-flier programs. All major U.S. airlines offer frequent-flier programs, which are free to join. Miles earned can be redeemed for upgrades from coach-class seats to business- or first-class. There are many opportunities to earn miles without flying — from hotels, car rental companies, credit cards and other businesses. *(A guide to frequent-flier programs, 12E.)*

Join an airport club. Road Warriors say being a member of an airport club is like having an office at the airport. Major airlines have networks of private clubs at U.S. and foreign airports they serve. Memberships cost a few hundred dollars a year but travelers get access to a private lounge where they can plug in their computer, send a fax or meet clients. *(Airport clubs, 10E.)*

Join a hotel frequent-guest program. Most are free. Earn points toward free room nights and upgrades to better rooms. You can also trade points for frequent-flier miles. Hotels have special check-in desks for members, so you don't have to wait in long lines to get into your room.

Keep a travel diary. A diary helps you remember when you've found a good place to eat or a nice hotel to stay at. Road Warrior Jody Samson keeps a book, alphabetized by city, that lists restaurant, hotel and sightseeing ideas. She says it's useful for business as well as pleasure trips.

Be prepared. Keep several pre-packed toiletries bags so you don't forget anything. One Road Warrior suggests keeping three sets of toiletries: one for home, one for short trips and one for long trips. *(Packing Guide, 11E.)*

Pack a snack. Bring your own food and water on airplanes in case food service is delayed because of mechanical or weather problems. Drink lots of water on the plane — and avoid alcohol — to keep from becoming dehydrated.

Carry a pager. A pager will help you stay in touch when you're on the road. Friends and family can reach you in emergencies. Road Warrior Jane-Ellen Miller got a message on her pager saying that she became an aunt.

Dress comfortably. Wear comfortable shoes and loose-fitting clothes to make getting around the airport or getting to your hotel easier and less stressful.

Carry a medical kit. For emergencies, take a safety kit with you that includes bandages, safety pins, aspirin, and medications to fight nausea and diarrhea.

Board the plane ASAP. Getting on the plane sooner instead of dawdling in the airport will leave you more time to find a place to store your bag, get a pillow and have your pick of magazines.

Overseas tips. Give yourself enough time to get your passport, which can take several weeks to process. Road Warriors suggest getting passports and visas through a travel agency that books a lot of international travel.

▶ Research business and social customs before you visit a foreign country.

▶ If you travel frequently to a particular country, have your business cards printed in English on one side and in that country's language on the other.

▶ At international hotels, introduce yourself to the concierge. They are an excellent source of information for travelers on local customs, how to get around a city, good places to eat and sights to see.

For more info ... write to the Department of Transportation for *Fly-Rights: A Consumer Guide to Air Travel*, Office of Consumer Affairs, I-25, 400 Seventh Street S.W., Washington, D.C. 20590.

By Donna Rosato

USA TODAY, 12 SEPTEMBER, 1995

DISCOVERY FILE

Hovering Choppers and Flights of Fancy

Thomas Edison once said that until aircraft could take off and land vertically, flight would not be practical.

Although the idea of vertical flight goes back centuries to a whirling Chinese propeller toy—the same flying top that fascinated the Wright brothers when they were boys—the first practical helicopters were invented in the 20th century.

The word *helicopter* comes from two Greek words meaning "spiral" and "wing." Leonardo da Vinci coined the word when he sketched plans in 1483 for an "airscrew," a flying machine that some people call his helicopter. Leonardo imagined that the machine would literally push its way through the air by means of its large vertical screws rotated by four men. Such a model would be too heavy for human-powered flight and would need a very powerful engine if it were to fly, concepts that Leonardo did not fully understand in the 15th century. His helicopter, imaginative as it was, can be said to be an "invention ahead of its time."

Although some early 19th-century inventors designed machines that lifted them off the ground for a few seconds, Russian-born aeronautical engineer Igor Sikorsky invented and flew the first successful helicopter in 1939. The distinctive "chop-chop" sound of a helicopter is what gave it the nickname of "chopper" later on, as it became a familiar sight on television news. The helicopter really came of age on the battlefields of the Korean and Vietnam Wars.

An airplane has fixed wings, but a helicopter's horizontal rotating blades—or rotor—can be said to be its "wings." The blades of a helicopter's rotor are in the shape of airfoils, like the wings of an airplane. The spinning blades produce lift when they rotate. But unlike a plane, the helicopter does not need a long runway on which to get up to speed before taking off. The helicopter can take off straight from the ground, in a vertical liftoff.

The blades of a rotor spin around, creating an area of low pressure above them. When their speed is great enough, they generate the lift that pushes up the craft upward. Rotor blades move quickly through the air. The body of the helicopter does not need to be moving forward for there to be lift. By varying the speed of the rotors and the *pitch*—angle—of the blades, the helicopter pilot can control the amount of lift.

Helicopters can move forward, backwards, sideways, and vertically. They can also hover. The direction the helicopter flies is determined by the pitch of the blades.

Helicopters with one main rotor will also have a tail rotor. The tail rotor prevents the fuselage from spinning around beneath the main rotor. Some helicopters have two main rotors to generate more lift and carry heavier loads.

Some other VTOL (Vertical TakeOff and Landing) aircraft have been developed since the original helicopter like the small autogyro, a small, rotary-winged aircraft. VTOL and STOL (Short TakeOff) capabilities have been used in several types of aircraft in recent times.

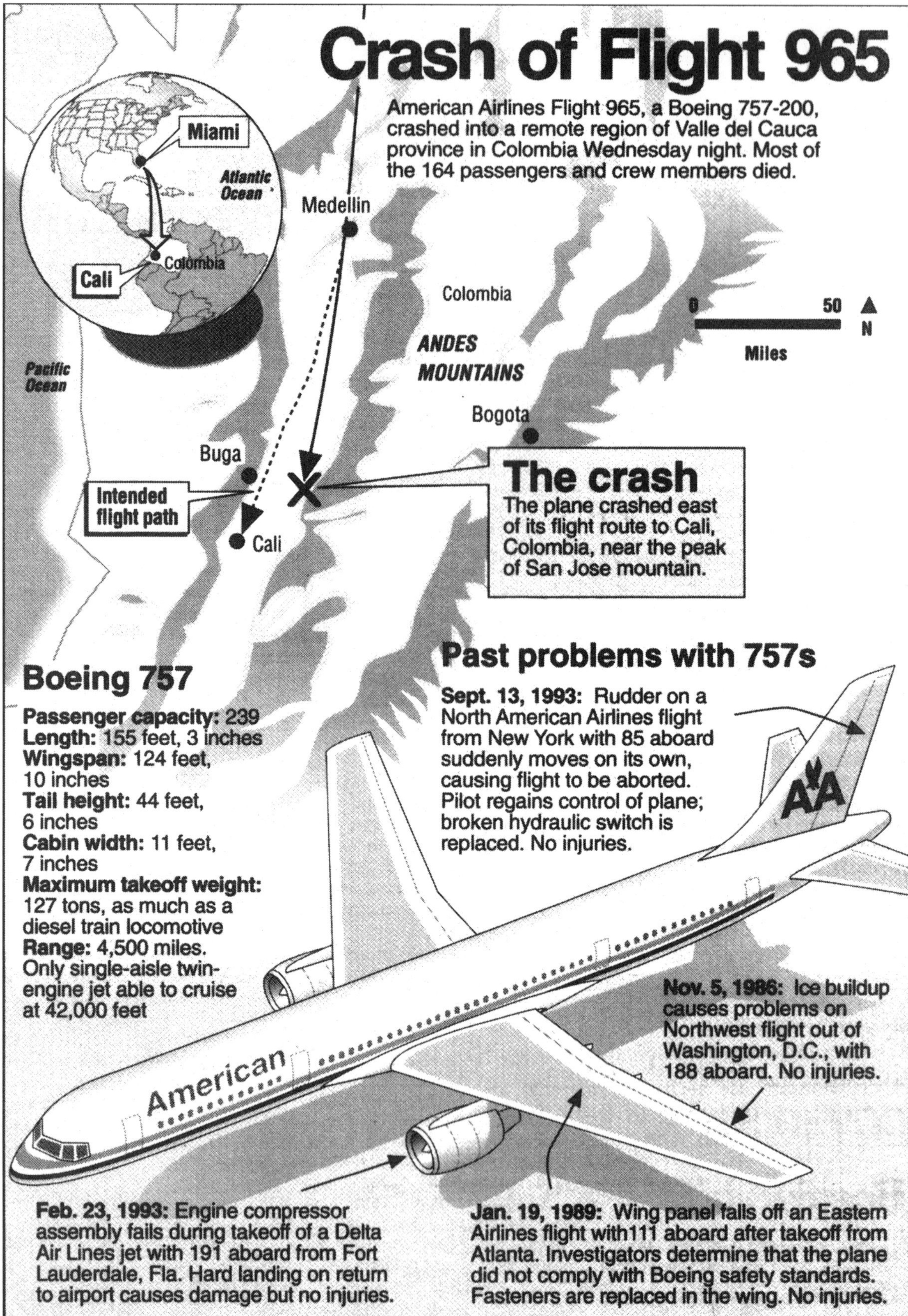

USA TODAY, 22 DECEMBER, 1995

The Story—Part 4

The Future of Flight

People have been flying for less than 100 years, yet ever since the first powered flight of the Wright brothers in 1903, they've tried to design and build faster and better planes.

The two World Wars saw many advances in aviation, including the invention of the jet engine. After World War II, the Cold War lead to further research and experiments in aviation.

In 1947, the era of supersonic flight began with the X-1, the first plane to fly faster than the speed of sound. It flew at Mach 1.06, at a top speed of 700 MPH. It was the first genuine supersonic plane and was piloted by Air Force Captain Charles E. "Chuck" Yeager. This was the first in a series of experimental research aircraft.

In the next 50 years, engineers designed increasingly faster aircraft, as well as planes that flew by solar power, aircraft that used human power, spacecraft that went to the moon and beyond, and many other experimental aircraft that never made the headlines but provided valuable lessons for the future of flight.

The X-34 was originally scheduled to make its first suborbital flight in 1998, but plans now are for 2000. Also in 2000, another experimental vehicle, the X-33, should be launched. The X-33 will take off like a rocket but land like an airplane. Developers hope that the X-33 aircraft will become the model for a cheaper, reusable space shuttle that might transport ordinary people to and from a space station.

As technology advances, as different materials become available, and more is learned about aeronautics, aircraft of the future may look very different from those flown today. Materials and design were critical to the development of *STEALTH* technology, for example. Composites are also making a difference.

Driven by the desire to fly faster and higher, aeronautical engineers will try new designs and new ways of building aircraft. The Boeing 777, for example, was designed entirely with computers.

PHOTO COURTESY OF NASA

The Concorde, the first supersonic aircraft to carry passengers, began regular service in 1976. Plans for a successor are on the drawing board. Another proposal is a commercial super jumbo jet that would carry 800 passengers, but before such a huge plane could fly, it would need more powerful engines to carry the additional weight. A "flying wing" design has been suggested for one such mega carrier.

The Airbus 320A series has another advance. It uses computers and something called a "fly-by-wire" system. Instead of using cables and hydraulic lines to physically operate control surfaces, Airbus computers send electronic signals. These signals activate motors that move those surfaces.

Advances in aviation are the result of much testing and building of models and prototypes. Not everyone is convinced that this experimentation and research is worth the cost. Some people feel that airplanes are not as efficient, or environmentally sound, as some other forms of transportation. Still others object to the billions of dollars spent on costly projects that would benefit only the limited number of passengers who could afford the higher expenses of flying costlier planes.

However, as long as people want to fly like the birds, or higher, creative and ingenious aeronautical engineers will continue pushing the envelope and soaring to new heights. Proposals are already out there for new aircraft that could fly as fast as Mach 25! Flying wings, solar-powered aircraft, and other aircraft as yet unimagined will be part of the future of flight.

INTERDISCIPLINARY ACTIVITY

English: Reading Historical Fiction

History can come alive when past events are used as the background for a novel. After thoroughly researching the factual information of a particular era, writers create sympathetic characters involved in realistic conflicts. Writers read newspaper articles from the time period, diaries, letters, and may even interview actual participants (or their ancestors) of an event. If you read a well-written piece of historical fiction, you will have a better understanding not only of facts but also of the relationships among historical, scientific, political, social, and personal concerns of the period.

For example, in the afterword of his novel *Dragonwings*, author Laurence Yep relates his fascination with newspaper accounts of a young Chinese flier, Fung Joe Guey, who flew a biplane in Oakland, California, on September 22, 1909. Although he only flew for twenty minutes before his biplane went down, he had improved upon the Wright brothers' original design and had plans to build a new biplane of steel pipes and silk. In *Dragonwings*, Yep creates a character based on Fung Joe Guey. He is Windrider, a Chinese immigrant who has the dream of building and flying a plane. His son, Moonshadow, tells the story of the fulfillment of his father's goal.

Read the following passage from *Dragonwings* (Chapter 11, pages 210 to 215 at end of first paragraph, *Dragonwings*, New York: HarperCollins Children's Books, 1975). When the narrator refers to the "demon year" and the "demon land," he is referring to Caucasians. After you have read the passage, answer the following questions:

1. What steps did Windrider take to build *Dragonwings?*
2. What obstacles did Windrider overcome in order to achieve his goal?
3. How would you compare the steps you have taken and the obstacles you have overcome to create your aircraft to Windrider's?

If you read the entire novel, you will learn more about Windrider's struggle as well as historical background about Chinese immigration to California in the early 1900s and the 1906 San Francisco earthquake.

English: Writing a Biographical Sketch

With a group of your classmates, brainstorm a list of people who have achieved notable success in their lifetimes. They may have been the first in their field to accomplish this achievement, like the Wright brothers, or they may have fulfilled a personal goal or dream, as illustrated in the lives of Olympic athletes. Perhaps someone you know, or you yourself may have accomplished an outstanding feat in a field such as academics, the arts, or sports.

Choose one of these subjects and research biographical information about him/her. Besides finding basic factual data, also search for character traits, obstacles that the subject had to overcome, and any material about the subject's feelings and attitudes. To find this information, you will have to use magazines, newspapers, television or personal interviews, and full-length biographies as well as encyclopedias. Be sure to use your own words as you take notes and list the sources of your information at the end of your paper. Your teacher will give you the correct form for listing your sources.

Now write your first draft using the information you have to create a profile of your subject. Although you may choose to organize your information in several different ways, beginning with a dramatic statement about the subject's accomplishment will capture your reader's attention. Remember, too, that your reader may not know who your subject is. Other paragraphs may highlight the subject's life, include quotations by or about the subject, or express your opinion of the subject.

After you have written your first draft, ask your peers to respond to your sketch, using the Peer Response Form on page 56. Continue to conference and revise until you are satisfied that you have the best possible profile. Finally, use the Proofreading Guidesheet on p. 57 to edit your sketch before submitting your final copy.

Mathematics: Warm Up

These warm up activities can be used in mathematics classes through the Event Based Science unit *First Flight!* Mathematics teachers can also use these as models to create their own warm up activities.

Use the graph below to answer questions 1 and 2.

1. Estimate the percent of surface air pressure at 3 km _____ ; at 15 km _____
2. Explain why the data are not graphed as a straight line.
3. The ratio of plane length to wingspan on a model for an aircraft prototype is 8 to 5. How long must the actual plane be if the wingspan is 38.5 feet?
4. Your model has a wing surface with an area of 60 cm^2. If the scale for the model is 1 cm = 1 meter, what will be the area of the wing surface for the actual plane?
5. Your friend Orville wants to fly you to San Francisco for the weekend. If his plane averages 400 miles per hour, how far will you travel if the flying time is 5 hours and 15 minutes?
6. Your flight to New York City leaves at 1:15 P.M., CST. You have to stop over at Cleveland for 20 minutes. The estimated time for the flight is 2:20 for the first leg and 1:35 for the second leg. Assuming that the airplane arrives on time, will you arrive in time to meet your aunt at the airport in New York at 6:20 P.M., EST? If so, how long will you have to wait for her? If not, how long will she have to wait for you?

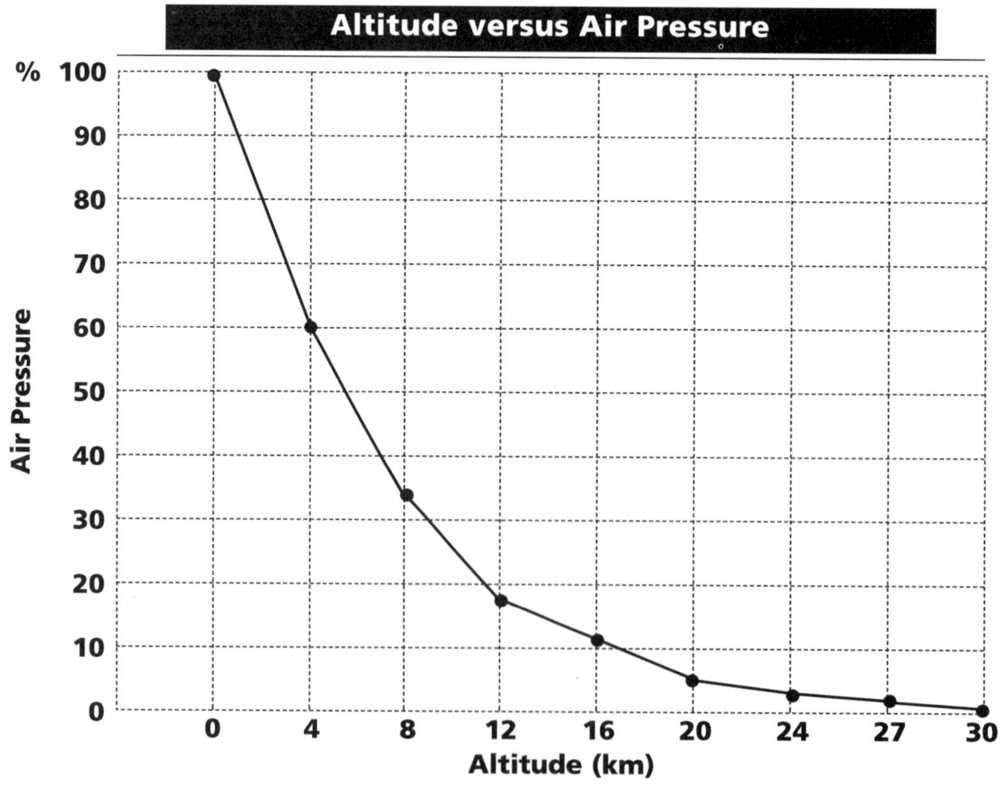

Mathematics: Flying Is Safer Than Picking Your Friends

Purpose

To investigate statistics comparing air safety to other common experiences.

Background

The sponsor of your community service club has been asked to provide students to talk to senior citizens about safety and air travel. You have received statistics from the National Transportation Safety Board and the National Highway Safety Administration. Research the information to prepare a telephone script for a conversation with a concerned potential traveler.

Procedure

Use the following information or more recent information from the Event-Based Science page on the World Wide Web to prepare a fact sheet for your telephone script. (http://mcps.k12.md.us/departments/eventscience/)

The total fatalities from accidents involving all scheduled U.S. airlines in 1994 was 264. In 1995 it was 175.

In 1994, 40,676 people lost their lives in car accidents. This represents an average of 111 people per day—one every 13 minutes! On average, a pedestrian is killed in an accident with a motor vehicle every 96 minutes.

The automobile fatality rate per 100 million vehicle miles was 1.7 in 1994. During the same period, the fatality rate per 100 million air miles was 0.0008.

In 1994 only one in about 1.7 million passengers died in a commercial airline accident. Over a 10-year period, the chance of being killed while flying was 1 in 3 million. It was 2.5 times more likely that you would be struck by lightning than die in an airplane crash.

Over 10 billion passengers have been transported by U.S. air carriers in the last 70 years, During this time, records show only 12,600 commercial-passenger fatalities. The long-term trend in air travel reflects a safety record of substantial and continuous improvement. This is quite encouraging as the next 10 billion passengers will be transported in a much shorter period—perhaps 12 years or less.

Using the facts provided, find the percent of decrease in air fatalities from 1994 to 1995.

1. Find the average number of people who died in an automobile accident in a month during 1994.
2. Find the number of people who were struck by lightning in 1994.
3. Find the ratio of car fatalities to air fatalities per mile. Be careful, both need the same units to compare.
4. Write a draft for a telephone script explaining the safety of air travel. Use the statistics provided to support your argument.

Social Studies: Win a Free Trip!

Purpose

To create a brochure advertising a tour of two foreign countries where travelers will examine similarities and differences between the cultures.

Materials

- map
- newspaper and magazine
- travel ads for airlines
- reference books
- lined paper
- sample travel brochures
- markers
- pens
- colored pencils

Background

You and three partners have been hired by a travel agency to design a trip for middle-school students. A nationally-known cereal company has provided the money for ten students and two chaperones to travel through two countries on a study tour. On the tour the students will compare and contrast different cultures while actually visiting the countries. Your travel agency is planning the trip and designing a brochure.

Procedure

You will work together with three other students to research the history and culture of two countries, plan an itinerary for the trip there, and select appropriate aircraft for the different legs of the trip. Be sure the stops include historic and cultural sites. The trip must focus on such aspects of each culture as government (past and present), art, religion, history, food (especially breakfast), agriculture, and anything else that seems appropriate to the country. Create a notebook and keep records of all the interesting things you find. Your brochure should focus on at least three similarities and three differences between the countries.

In addition, create a workbook of questions for the students to answer as they travel. Give them questions for each point on their trip. Be sure to include specific questions about each of the places you send them. Create a conclusion page where they can compare and contrast things about the countries. Prepare a "suggested answer" key for the chaperones.

Before you design your brochure, you should examine several real brochures from travel agencies. Ask a travel agent about the kinds of airplanes that are available to get students from your city to the first country. Plan to use the largest airplane available. Find out how much time is involved so you can list it in your brochure. Plan ground transportation from the airport to the first hotel, and to all sites in the first country.

Use a smaller plane from the first country to the second. Find out how long that flight takes and list it in the brochure too. Plan ground transportation and hotel accommodations for the students.

Conclusion

Your final products include a brochure that contains a detailed itinerary. It should include maps so students know where they are on any day. Attach the workbook containing study questions, to the answer key. Place your final package in an envelope for mailing to the cereal company.

Writing to Persuade

Purpose
To demonstrate knowledge of lift, thrust, and air safety and the persuasive writing style in an essay to your younger brother

Background
Your family is about to take an airplane trip to a far away resort. You have flown before and are looking forward to flying again. But your younger brother has never been on an airplane.

Materials
- Discovery File "Four Forces in Flight" (page 24)
- Discovery File "Bernoulli's Famous Principle" (page 23)
- Discovery File "Flight Safety: The Story Statistics Tell" (page 44)
- In the News articles on overcoming fear of flying (pages 6–7)
- Copy of Peer-Response Form (page 56)
- Proofreading Guidesheet (page 57)
- Student Voices

Prompt
Your younger brother says he will not go! He says he wants to do all the wonderful things that you can do at the resort, but he still doesn't want to go. Your parents have talked to him and found that he is afraid to fly. They tried everything. Now it's up to you!

As the oldest child in your family, your parents have asked you to help persuade your younger brother that flying in an airplane is as safe as driving in a car—probably safer. You know that if you cannot persuade him, the trip is off, so you want to plan the case you will present very carefully. The important points you want to make include how lift supports the weight of a plane, and how safe air travel is. This discussion is so important that you decide to write out your explanation before you confront your little brother.

Begin with an introduction that gets your brother's attention. Explain what lift is and tell how it's created. State two or three activities that are less safe than flying. Use facts and data from science activities and discovery files to support your statements.

Finally, write a brief conclusion that sums up your points and tells some of the fun things you will miss out on if your brother doesn't change his mind. And remember, if persuasion fails bribery has worked with your brother in the past.

An exceptional argument:
- Has an attention-getting introduction.
- Clearly states an opinion.
- Gives facts to support the opinion.
- Has a strong conclusion.
- Is relatively error-free and follows the conventions of grammar.

Use the Proofreading Guidesheet on page 57 to edit your letter. Have your peers evaluate and react to your letter using a copy of the Peer-Response Form on page 56.

Questions
1. How do you get your brother's attention?
2. How and where is your opinion stated?
3. What information about lift, wing design, and attack angle do you include? What other information might you include?
4. What data and facts do you use to support your opinion.
5. What other data might you use?
6. How could you improve your conclusion to make it stronger?

Peer-Response Form

Directions

1. Ask your partners to listen carefully as you read your rough draft aloud.
2. Ask your partners to help you improve your writing by telling you their answers to the questions below.
3. Jot down notes about what your partners say:

   a. What did you like best about my rough draft?

   b. What did you have the hardest time understanding in my rough draft?

   c. What can you suggest that I do to improve my rough draft?

4. Exchange rough drafts with a partner. In pencil, place a check mark near any mechanical, spelling, punctuation, or grammatical constructions about which you are uncertain. Return the papers and check your own. Ask your partner for clarification if you do not understand or agree with the comments on your paper. Jot down notes you want to remember when writing your revision.

Proofreading Guidesheet

1. Have you identified the assigned purpose of the writing assignment? Have you accomplished this purpose?
2. Have you written on the assigned topic?
3. Have you identified the assigned form your writing should take? Have you written accordingly?
4. Have you addressed the assigned audience in your writing?
5. Have you used sentences of different lengths and types to make your writing effective?
6. Have you chosen language carefully so the reader understands what you mean?
7. Have you done the following to make your writing clear for someone else to read?

- used appropriate capitalization
- kept pronouns clear
- kept verb tense consistent
- used correct spelling
- used correct punctuation
- used complete sentences
- made all subjects and verbs agree
- organized your ideas into logical paragraphs

APPENDIX

Aviation Time Line

Before Recorded History
People have probably always dreamed of flying. Discoveries of some flight principles may have occurred in ancient times. For instance, a child's toy (dating from about 300 B.C.) was discovered in Egypt: a bird with tapering wings carved in a distinct airfoil pattern, with evidence that it had a horizontal tail.

Myths and Legends
Many cultures have had myths of people or gods that fly. In ancient Greek legend Daedalus built a great labyrinth for King Minos of Crete. King Minos imprisoned him so that he would not reveal the secret of the labyrinth. Daedalus escaped with his son Icarus by making feather and wax wings and flying away. But in the joy of soaring, Icarus flew too close to the sun, the wax on his wings melted, and he plunged into the sea.

3,000 years ago, China
The Chinese invented and flew kites at least 3,000 years ago. Kites eventually reached Europe in the 14th century. Although we think of them primarily as toys, they have been used to lift people for serious observations, for measurement or weaponry in war, and today for meteorological work. Marco Polo witnessed kites carrying humans in China in the 1300s.

400 B.C., Greece
Archytas of Tarentum, a Greek mathematician, scientist, and philosopher who lived in Italy, may have designed a small flying "dove" balanced so as to fly by means of a whirling arm that provided lift.

Middle Ages, Europe
Roger Bacon, an English Franciscan monk, suggested the use of large, hollow globes of thin metal, filled with rarefied air or "liquid fire" (perhaps hydrogen gas) to achieve flight. Most experimenters, however, just designed wings, strapped them on, and jumped. As far as we know, none of them worked. Some of the would-be aviators died. Children played with toy helicopters. This may have been true of children on many continents.

1010, England
An English monk, Eilmer, jumped from Malmesbury Abbey equipped with flapping wings. He broke his legs.

1162, Constantinople
A man in Constantinople tried to fly from the top of a tower using sail-like wings made of pleated fabric. He did not survive.

1400s, Italy
Leonardo da Vinci applied his extraordinary mind to understanding flight by carefully studying birds. He realized human arms are too weak to flap wings for long, so he sketched designs for machines with wings that would flap. The power was supplied by a person winding levers with his hands and pushing on pedals with his feet. Leonardo never built the ornithopter. If he had, it wouldn't have flown anyway. Leonardo didn't understand enough about how birds fly, and the materials available in his time were far too heavy. However, his was among the first scientific efforts to design a flying machine. He invented the airscrew and designed the first real parachute (hand-held size) in history.

1600s, Turkey
Hezarfen Celebi leapt from a tower at Galata and flew some distance before landing safely in the marketplace of Scutari.

1678, France
A French locksmith named Besnier tried to fly with wings modeled after the webbed feet of a duck. He was lucky—he survived.

1709, Portugal
Father Bartolomeu de Gusmao demonstrated a model hot air balloon to King John V and others. It was made of paper and inflated by heated air from burning materials carried in a suspended earthenware bowl.

1783, France
The world's first manned balloon flight occurred on November 21, 1783 over Paris, astonishing the population. The balloon was designed by the brothers Joseph and Jacques-Etienne Montgolfier. Jean

Pilatre de Rozier and the Marquis d'Arlandes rode in it. It was made of linen and paper and lifted by heated air.

1783, France
Jacques Charles and M. Robert made the second balloon flight in history, also over Paris. Their balloon was made of rubberized silk and filled with hydrogen gas instead of hot air. Hydrogen gas was more practical since it didn't have to be heated in flight.

1797, France
Andre Jacques Garnerin landed safely by the use of a parachute after jumping from a balloon at approximately 2,000 feet (600 m).

1799, England
Sir George Cayley invented the concept of the fixed-wing aircraft. Modern airplane design is based on his ideas.

1804, England
Sir George Cayley conducted experiments with kites to understand how things fly. While many people believed that flying would develop through lighter-than-air craft, he was convinced that one day wings would carry people in the air. One of his great contributions was to separate the ideas of lift, propulsion, and control (a bird's wings provide all three, unlike man-made aircraft). From his work with kites he learned so much about how things are lifted in the air that he was able to build a glider. His glider is the basis for modern aircraft design.

1819, Paris
Marie Madeleine Sophie Blanchard, wife of balloonist Jean-Pierre Blanchard, a capable aeronaut and chief of Napoleon's air service, lost her life when her hydrogen balloon caught fire as she watched a fireworks display. She was the first woman to lose her life while flying.

1845, England
William Henson and John Stringfellow built a working model of a plane powered by a specially made, lightweight steam engine. It did not fly. Over the next decades many imaginative people tried to build steam-powered flying machines. But the engines were either too weak or too heavy. Powered flight wasn't possible until the invention of the powerful, compact, gasoline engine.

1852, France
Henri Giffard addressed the great limitation of balloons—they would float wherever the wind took them. He made a cigar-shaped balloon and powered it with a steam engine to make it "dirigible," that is, steerable. This was the first manned, powered, steerable aircraft.

1853, England
Sir George Cayley built a full-size glider. It supposedly carried his terrified coachman across a small valley.

Late 1800s, Western Europe
Balloons became fashionable and popular. Men competed for distance and height records. Balloon races were generally thought unsuitable for women who were considered too delicate for this sport. People who raced balloons also had to be well off—it took time and money to participate in this hobby.

1890s, Germany
Otto Lilienthal built a series of small, fragile gliders. He adopted a scientific approach: he studied each problem carefully and tested each solution. In his gliders he supported himself on his forearms, and steered by swinging his legs to shift his center of gravity. He succeeded in making the first regular, controlled flights with his gliders. Lilienthal discovered that a curved, or "cambered" wing surface creates the best lift. He was killed in 1896 when a gust of wind threw his glider out of control.

1890, France
French engineer Clement Ader built a steam plane—an airplane powered by a lightweight steam engine. It flew 164 feet (50 m) in a straight line. Since there was no control, Clement Ader's flight is not considered a real flight. Notably, his plane took off from level ground, not needing a slope to gain speed.

1896, United States
Samuel Langley achieved sustained, powered flight, but his heavier-than-air Aerodrome had no pilot on board.

1903, Kitty Hawk, North Carolina, USA
Orville and Wilbur Wright flew a gasoline-powered flying machine about 120 feet (37 m), for 12 seconds, over the sands at Kitty Hawk, North Carolina, and returned safely to the ground. It was the world's first successful, piloted, powered flight. Orville was the pilot. That short flight is

widely considered the starting point of modern aviation. The Wright brothers made four flights that day. The last, with Wilbur as pilot, flew 59 seconds and 852 feet (260 m). Their aircraft, the *Flyer,* can now be seen at the Smithsonian's National Air and Space Museum, Washington, D.C. The Wright brothers' success came about in part because of their thorough preparation. Wilbur once wrote: "Having set out with absolute faith in the existing scientific data, we were driven to doubt one thing after another, until finally, after two years of experiment, we cast it all aside, and decided to rely entirely upon our own investigations." They tested many designs, and improved their flying skill with each one. They used a wind tunnel to do practical tests of their propellers, and wings. For a brief time they were far ahead of all other pioneers, but so many people were interested in flying that progress was rapid everywhere.

1906, France
Alberto Santos-Dumont of Brazil made the first sustained airplane flight in Europe: 197 feet (59 m) in a straight line, about 10 feet (3 m) above the ground. Only a few months later, he flew 722 feet (217m) in 21 seconds, winning a prize for the first European flight covering more than 100 meters.

1907, France
Paul Cornu, a French mechanic, flew briefly in a primitive aircraft that was lifted by two horizontally-rotating wings—the first helicopter. Helicopters proved so unstable that they were not reliable aircraft until the flight of the first autogiro in 1923.

1908, Italy
Madame Thèrese Peltier was the first woman to fly solo in an airplane.

1908, England
Muriel Matters, a suffragette and balloonist, flew over the British Houses of Parliament dropping hundreds of flyers urging "votes for women." It was possibly the first use of the air for political lobbying and publicity.

1908, England
Famous author H. G. Wells wrote "War in the Air," a story envisioning the colossal destruction wrought by aerial bombing.

1909, France
Louis Blériot flew a small aircraft 26 miles (42 km) over the channel from France to England. His aircraft were monoplanes (single wing) with a separate tail. He adopted the Wright brothers' technique of "warping" the wings—using wires to twist the wings and lift one side or the other. This allowed controlled turns. After his crossing of the Channel, Blériot became a celebrity. He was cheered in London, and by a crowd of over 100,000 people when he returned to Paris. His flight fired the public imagination and also immediately began to worry governments, which became concerned about the power and protection of their navys. Blériot set a speed record in 1909 of 48 mph (77 kph). More than 100 of Blériot's Type XI aircraft were ordered. He became the world's first large-scale aircraft manufacturer.

1909, France
The world's first international air show was held in Reims. The planes were mostly made of wood. They could climb as high as 500 feet (150 m) above the ground. The fastest airplane in the show flew 47 mph (75 kph). Within four years, aircraft were flying over 120 mph (192 kph), climbing as high as 20,000 feet (6,000 m), and performing aerobatic feats such as loops and rolls.

1909, United States
The U.S. Army buys its first plane.

1910, France
The colorful, self-styled Baroness Raymonde de Laroche, an artist and car driver, became the first woman officially qualified as a pilot. She received pilot's certificate #36.

1910 - 1929, United States
The Barnstorming Era. Stunt flyers and exhibition teams put on shows and introduced thousands of people to the idea of flying. For a fee, they would take passengers up for a brief flight. Their shows included loops, rolls, daredevil stunts close to the ground, parachute jumping, and wingwalking.

Barnstorming was dangerous. Many pilots lost their lives. Some of the better known were Harriet Quimby, Bessie Coleman, Katherine and Eddie Stinson (Eddie was the first pilot to discover how to recover a plane from a spin), and Charles Lindbergh.

1910, Europe
Jorge Chavez, a Peruvian, became the first to fly an aeroplane over the Alps. Unfortunately just as he was about to land and complete his great feat, one of his aircraft's wings buckled. He crashed and did not survive.

1911, United States
Harriet Quimby became the first American woman to receive a pilot's license. She was one of the most celebrated stunt pilots of the early years of flight. The second woman to receive a license was her good friend, Mathilde Moissant.

1911, United States
Calbraith Rodgers became the first person to cross the continent in a plane. He was followed by a train carrying a mechanic, his wife, and spare parts for his plane. The plane crashed 19 times. The trip took 49 days and Rodgers arrived with one leg in a cast. He was cheered by a crowd of 20,000 people in Pasadena, California, when he arrived.

1911, France
The first women's flying school was founded in France, run by qualified pilot Jane Herveux.

1911, United States
Eugene Ely, test pilot for the Curtiss Company, did the first landing on a warship at sea. In order to stop fast enough, a system of ropes stretched across a platform and secured to sandbags was used to aid in braking.

1911, Ireland
Lilian Bland designed, built, and flew a plane—the first powered aircraft to be built in Ireland. She had always been fascinated by birds and flight. After Blériot's famous crossing of the English channel, she became determined to learn to fly. She attended an aviation meeting and studied the flying machines there. Later, she returned home and built her airplane, which she whimsically named the *Mayfly*.

1911, Germany
Melli Beese was about to take her test flight to gain her pilot's license when she discovered that some of her male colleagues so disliked the idea of a woman learning to fly that they drained her aircraft's fuel tanks and even tampered with the steering mechanism. She managed to take her test that day, however, and gained her license in spite of them.

1913, China
China bought its first fleet of aircraft and opened a flying school in Beijing.

1914, United States
The first regularly scheduled passenger service began operating between St. Petersburg and Tampa, Florida. The fare was $5.00 one way for up to 200 pounds of both passenger and baggage.

1914–1918 World War I
The military need for observation planes and fighter planes to use in the war pushed the improvement of the airplane. World War I was the first major conflict involving the use of air power. By the end of the war, the airplane had become fairly reliable and maneuverable. Hinged wing flaps called *ailerons* soon replaced the Wright brother's "wing warping" system for banking into a turn. Because of a wood shortage, manufacturers began to use metal in their airplanes. Early in the war, biplanes were popular. Their second wing gave them added lift and stability. As monoplanes were improved, they became more popular. One wing meant less drag.

During this time, dirigibles were also developed and used, particularly by Germany. However, they became less important as airplanes continued to improve.

1916, United States
The Boeing Aircraft Company was founded by William Boeing, a timber merchant. It began as the Pacific Aero Products Company, and is still a highly-successful airplane manufacturer today.

1916, United States
Ruth Law broke the American nonstop-distance record, flying 590 miles from Chicago to Hormel, New York. To survive the cold in her open cockpit, she wore four complete suits of wool and leather clothes.

1917, United States
Katherine Stinson broke Ruth Law's distance record by flying 610 miles (976 km) nonstop.

1918, United States
The first U.S. attempt to transport mail by air occurred on May 15, 1918. It was not a success—the pilot got lost.

1918, United States
Congress formed NACA, the National Advisory Committee on Aeronautics. NACA later became NASA, the National Aeronautics and Space Administration.

1918
Louis C. Candelaria of Argentina made the first successful flight of an airplane over the Andes, the highest mountain range in the western hemisphere. He took off from Zapala in Argentina and landed in Cunco, Chile.

1919, Canada/Ireland
The first successful, nonstop, transatlantic airplane flight was made by British fliers Captain John Alcock (pilot) and Arthur Whitten-Brown (navigator). They flew from Newfoundland to Ireland, braving darkness, clouds, sleet, and snow.

1919, U.S./Canada
The first international airmail was flown between the United States and Canada.

1919 U.S./Cuba
Aeromarine Airways became the first international airline flying scheduled flights out of the United States. It flew between Key West and Havana.

1921, Argentina
Adrienne Bolland became the first woman to fly over the Andes. She took off from Mendoza, Argentina, and landed 10 hours later in Santiago de Chile. Huge crowds greeted her arrival. She had flown at an altitude of 14,750 feet, braving the bitter cold and having to avoid mountain peaks that were higher than her airplane could fly.

1923, Spain
Juan de la Cierva of Spain crossed the English Channel in the world's first autogyro, a craft that uses a propeller for forward movement and a rotor for lift.

1925
The trial of Col. William "Billy" Mitchell. A hero of the great war (World War I), he was court-martialed for making public statements "contrary to military order and discipline." The outspoken Mitchell angered his superiors not only because of his harsh manner, but because he insisted that the U.S. Armed Forces devote more resources to the U.S. Army Air Service and make it a separate arm equal to the Army and the Navy. When several Naval aircraft crashed after long flights, Mitchell stated publically that the crashes were caused by "incompetence, criminal negligence, and almost treasonable" actions by members of the Army and Navy. Years after his trial he was posthumously honored for his vision and achievements.

1926, North Pole
United States Navy Commander Richard Byrd navigated while his pilot Floyd Bennett flew over the North Pole for the first time. This aviation first has been challenged in recent years.

1927, United States/France
Charles Lindbergh flew the first nonstop, solo flight from New York to Paris in his plane, the *Spirit of St. Louis.* He was cheered by huge crowds when he landed in Paris. A few weeks later, when he returned to the United States, over a million people lined the streets of New York to cheer him during a ticker-tape parade.

1930, United States
Flying for United Airlines, Ellen Church became the world's first airline stewardess. She was a registered nurse, as were the next eight stewardesses hired by United. They wore white nurses' uniforms while on duty.

1930, United States
Ruth Nichols set a transcontinental speed record of 13 hours and 21 minutes, beating a previous record set by Charles Lindbergh.

1930, India
Amy Johnson, an English woman, set a speed record flying from London to India in 13 days. She then continued her flight and eventually reached her destination in Australia, where she was greeted by cheering crowds. When she saw the crowds from the air, she thought she must have arrived during an air pageant, not realizing they were there to greet her.

1933, Around the World
Wiley Post of the U.S. set a record flying the first solo flight around the world—15,596 miles (24,954 km) in 7 days, 19 hours. Post and his navigator Harold Gatty flew around the Northern Hemisphere, crossing the Atlantic, parts of Europe, the USSR, Alaska, and Canada.

1933, United States
The first modern airliner, the Boeing 247, was placed in service. An all-metal, twin-engine airplane, the 247 was the first passenger airliner with an autopilot, pneumatically operated de-icing equipment, a variable-pitch propeller, and retractable landing gear.

1933, Spain/Cuba
Mariaon Barberan and Joaquin Collar made the first nonstop

flight between Seville, Spain, and Cuba. It was the first crossing of the Atlantic to the West Indies.

1937, United States
The luxury airship *Hindenberg* exploded in Lakehurst, New Jersey. The dramatic fire and the deaths of 36 people on board marked the end of the era of huge dirigibles.

1937, Japan/England
To mark the coronation of England's King George VI, Japanese pilot Masaaki Iinuma and navigator Kenji Tsukagoshi flew from Japan to England in just under four days. Eager crowds welcomed the aviators.

1937, Spain
The town of Guernica, Spain, was the scene of massive bombing from the air by German aircraft. The raid, which lasted four hours and left much of the population dead and most of the town destroyed, was ostensibly to destroy a bridge. The bridge was undamaged. It was the worst such attack in history up to that date.

1939–1945 World War II
Need for aircraft for military superiority fueled the development of faster and more efficient fighter planes, transport planes, radar and navigation systems, helicopters, and jets. Air power, as predicted by Billy Mitchell so many years before, was a decisive factor in the waging of this war.

1939, Germany
Test pilot Erich Warsitz made the first jet flight, in a German Heinkel He 178.

1941, United States
Formation of the Tuskegee Airmen, the first African-American fighter squadron in the U.S. armed forces. Until 1941, African Americans had been forbidden from receiving pilot training.

1943, United States
The Women Airforce Service Pilots (WASPS) were formed to ferry military planes and perfom other noncombat operations for the U.S. military during World War II. They flew with distinction but were disbanded as the war ended because opposition to women military pilots was so great.

1947, United States
U.S. Air Force test pilot Chuck Yeager broke the sound barrier flying in a Bell X-1 rocket powered aircraft. He flew at a speed of 1,127 kilometers (700 miles) per hour, Mach 1.06, at an altitude of 13,000 meters (43,000 feet).

1948, United States
The world's first flying car was flown. The Hall flying automobile was an automobile with a detachable airplane wing and a tail.

1948, United States
Record for the decade for speed set by Amy Johnson, flying 671 mph (1,073 kph).

1948, United States
President Harry S. Truman signed the executive order desegregating the armed forces of the United States.

1953, United States
Jacqueline Cochran became the first woman to fly faster than sound. She was one of the most admired aviators in the United States. By the time of her death in 1980, she held more records for speed and distance than any other pilot before or since.

1959, USSR
Speed record for the decade set by Mosolov, flying 1,483.51 mph.

1959, Around the World
First around-the-world jet passenger service was offered by Pan American Airways in a Boeing 707.

1961, United States
Ross and Prather set a balloon altitude record of 113,740 feet (34,122 m).

1963, United States
NASA pilot Joseph Walker flew the experimental X-15 rocket airplane to a record altitude of 67 miles (108 km). The X-15 was launched from beneath the wing of a modified B-52 bomber.

1964, United States
Jerrie Mock was the first woman to fly solo around the world. The flight, in a Cessna 18, lasted 29 days.

1967
The first automatic landing by a jet was made by a Boeing 707.

1969, United States
The test flight of the Boeing 747, the first wide-bodied jumbo jet, was conducted. The 747 has been a highly successful commercial aircraft. The challenge in its design was the scale-up of an aircraft to this size. Boeing

747s typically carry 420 passengers. They have a maximum range of 8320 miles (13,390 km).

1969, France and Great Britain
Flight of the *Concorde,* the first commercial airplane capable of traveling faster than the speed of sound. The *Concorde* travels at Mach 2.2, and is used primarily by business travelers.

1971, Great Britain
Sheila Scott made the first flight equator-to-equator over the North Pole.

1971, United States
Elgin Long made the first around-the-world flight over the poles in a Piper Navajo, travelling 38,896 miles (62,234 km) in 215 hours.

1979, English Channel
First human-powered flight across the English Channel by Paul MacCready in the *Gossamer Albatross.* The aircraft weighed only 200 lbs. (90 kg), and had wings nearly 100 feet (30 m) long.

1981, United States
U.S. Astronauts John Young and Robert Crippen piloted the space shuttle Columbia on its maiden flight from Kennedy Space Center in Florida, marking the first flight into orbit of America's resuable "space plane"—part rocket and part glider. The flight ended with a perfect reentry and landing at Edwards Air Force Base in California.

1986, United States
Dick Rutan and Jeana Yeager set a distance record for airplanes and made the first (and so far, the only) nonstop, non-refueled, around-the-globe flight in their frail plane, the *Voyager.* They flew 24,987 miles (39,979 km) in 9 days, 3 minutes, 44 seconds.

1987, United States
First over-the-poles, around-the-world flight by a single-engine plane made by Norton and Rosetti in a Piper Malibu, flying 34,342 miles (54,947 km) in 185 hours, 41 minutes.

1988, United States
Longest flight by a human-powered aircraft made by Kanellos Kanellopoulos in the MIT-built aircraft the *Daedalus.* The *Daedalus* flew the 74 miles (118 km) from Crete to Santorini Island over the Mediterranean Sea.

1988, Austria
Distance record for an ultralight was set by Lischak, flying 1,011 miles (1618 km).

1991
Longest balloon flight ever, by the *Virgin Otsuka Pacific Flyer,* 6,761 miles (10,818 km).

1994
Vicki Van Meter was 12 years old when she flew a Cessna 210 across the Atlantic, becoming the youngest pilot to ever make a transatlantic flight.

1994
Test flight of the Boeing 777, the first aircraft designed entirely on a computer.

Acknowledgments

Author
Russell G. Wright, with contributions from Louise Wile, Janet Wert Crampton, and the following Montgomery County Public School teachers:

Science Activities
William R. Krayer
Gaithersburg High School*
Gaithersburg, MD
Frank S. Weisel
Tilden Middle School*
North Bethesda, MD

Teacher Advisors
Joyce Bailey
Julius West Middle School*
Rockville, MD
Katherine Bender
Montgomery Village Middle School*
Gaithersburg, MD
Patricia L. Berard
Colonel E. Brooke Lee Middle School*
Silver Spring, MD
Barbara Deitsch
T. W. Pyle Middle School*
Bethesda, MD
Chris Grant
Roberto Clemente Middle School*
Germantown, MD
Eugene M. Molesky
Ridgeview Middle School*
Gaithersburg, MD
Michelle Smetanick
Ridgeview Middle School*
Gaithersburg, MD
Thomas G. Smith
Briggs Chaney Middle School*
Silver Spring, MD
Kay Steiger
Westland Middle School*
Bethesda, MD
Barbara L. Teichman
Parkland Middle School*
Rockville, MD

Interns
Lauren Bascom
Grove City College
Grove City, PA
Susan Buffington
Salisbury State University
Salisbury, MD
Seth Kruglak
University of Pennsylvania
Philidelphia, PA
Ben Schulman
George Washington University
Washington, DC

Interdisciplinary Activities
James J. Deligianis
Tilden Middle School*
North Bethesda, MD
Lauren Bascom
Grove City College
Grove City, PA
Phyllis Vestal
Gaithersburg Middle School*
Gaithersburg, MD

Event-Site Support
EllaJay Parfitt
Southeast Middle School
Baltimore, MD

Scientific Reviewers
Dorothy K. Hall
National Aeronautics and Space Administration

In addition, the following Montgomery County Public School students served as consultants on this unit:

Tilden Middle School*, Rockville, MD:
Lisa Aronoff, Javi Baquero, Ariana Berengaut, Isaac Breslaw, Pamela Corbett, Tiziana DiFabio, Erika Fardig, Michelle Glowa, Jeffrey Hall, Clara Meade, David Messner, Alexandra Nemcocky, Alexey Rostapshov, Andrew Tingley, Kira VanNiel, Jean Yi

Field test teachers:
Patricia Flynn
Agawam Jr. High
Feeding Hills, MA
Beverly Franzoy
Hatch Middle School
Hatch, NM
Veryl Howard
Backus Middle School
Washington, DC
Helen Linn
Cathy Miller
Huron Middle School
Northglenn, CO
George Head
Kirtland Middle School
Kirtland, NM
Cheryl Glotfelty
Darren Wilburn
Northern Middle School
Accident, MD
Festus Vanjah
Renekki Wilson
Roper Middle School
Washington, DC
Wendy Beavis
Mike Geil
Tanana Middle School
Fairbanks, AK

*Asterisks indicate Montgomery County Schools

EBS Advisory Committee

Dr. Joseph Antensen
Baltimore City Public Schools

Ms. Deanna Beane
Association of Science-Technology Centers

Ms. MaryAnn Brearton
AAAS - Project 2061

Dr. Jack Cairns
Delaware Department of Public Instruction

Dr. Gerard Consuegra
Montgomery County Public Schools

Mr. Bob Dubill and Ms. Robin Cherry
USA Today

Mr. Gary Heath
Maryland State Department of Education

Dr. Henry Heikkinen
University of Northern Colorado

Dr. Ramon Lopez
American Physical Society

Dr. J. David Lockard
University of Maryland (Emeritus)

Dr. Wayne Moyer
Montgomery County Public Schools (Retired)

Dr. Arthur Popper
University of Maryland